李清照诗词英译全集

COMPLETE COLLECTION OF LI QINGZHAO'S POETRY TRANSLATED

BY MANFIELD ZHU

朱曼华 编译

商务印书馆国际有限公司

图书在版编目（CIP）数据

李清照诗词英译全集：汉英对照 / 朱曼华编译．—
北京：商务印书馆国际有限公司，2018.11
ISBN 978-7-5176-0606-2

Ⅰ．①李… Ⅱ．①朱… Ⅲ．①英语－汉语－对照读物
②宋词－选集 Ⅳ．① H319.4：I

中国版本图书馆 CIP 数据核字 (2018) 第 230559 号

Complete Collection of Li Qingzhao's Poetry Translated by Manfield Zhu
李清照诗词英译全集

编　　译　朱曼华
责任编辑　庞洪斌　于　洋
封面设计　武守友
出版发行　商务印书馆国际有限公司
地　　址　北京市东城区史家胡同甲 24 号（邮编 100010）
电　　话　010-65592876（总编室）010-65277378（编辑部）
　　　　　010-65598498（市场营销部）
网　　址　www.cpi1993.com
经　　销　全国新华书店
印　　刷　北京中科印刷有限公司
开　　本　710mm × 1000mm　1/16
印　　张　12
字　　数　210 千字
版　　次　2018 年 11 月第 1 版第 1 次印刷
书　　号　ISBN 978-7-5176-0606-2
定　　价　35.00 元

序 言

1987年到2009年，我在欧美同学会工作。负责联系留美分会，编辑出版《欧美同学会会刊》（后更名为《留学生》杂志和《欧美同学会通讯》）。从那时起，开始接触朱曼华学长。

朱曼华学长曾留学美国伊利诺伊大学，是首都经贸大学教授，中国译协资深翻译家，并曾兼任留美分会副会长。他热心会务工作，经常为杂志和通讯撰稿。他英译的散文、诗歌、杂文以及反映会员活动的通讯报道总是那么及时地放在我的案头。

大家都称道他才思敏捷，笔力劲道，有时还兼有一丝诙谐。记得他曾多次指出翻译家王佐良、杨宪益、戴乃迪等人译文中的谬误。例如，在《红楼梦》英译本的“四季诗”中，译者杨宪益竟然把“蟆更”（古时夜里打木梆子报时，相当于五更，是文武百官上早朝的时段）英译为 frogs’ croaking（“青蛙呱呱叫”）。当时《红楼梦》英译本出版已27年，作为大学英语精读的范本，一直无人发现这样的错误。《欧美同学会会刊》发表了朱曼华学长为此所撰写的文章，包括他修改后重新英译的含“春夏秋冬”的四首以贾宝玉名义所写的格律诗，我着实为他的勇气和求真务实感叹。在后来很长一段时间里，他的一些文字总是让我先看。

2012年，我编辑了他《中国历代诗词英译集锦》一书的初稿。2013年该书由商务印书馆国际有限公司出版，2016年再版，成为译界为数不多的畅销书。2014年，他完成了《李煜诗词英译全集》书稿，特意请我为这本新作写了几句话。近日欣闻这本书6月份刚刚出版两个月后又马上要加印，很为他高兴。

经过不懈的耕耘，时下他又完成了《李清照诗词英译全集》一书的编译。他说，这是他最不敢轻易出手的书稿。因为英译李清照名诗词的人太多了，翻译高手也太多了。如果译作没有什么特色，还不如不出。实际上，这本书稿在他手里已经压了一年多，一改再改，总不满意。他不止一次地谈及，编译《李清照诗词英译全集》所花的时间和心思远远多于前两本译作，他希望能对得起自己和读者。为此，他在“译注”中从全新的角度诠释了李清照的生平和诗词意境。希望他的英译，不仅仅是摆在李清照西窗前的花瓶，而是能照亮她内心的红烛；希望他的文字，是展示李清照这位中国杰出女词人的廊桥，给所有步入的行人带来美好。

最后，我特别想说的是他的译诗像诗，这是他英译的特点。他非常注意母语为英语的老师和同学对他英译的反馈，力求真实评估英译效果，从不自以为是。如果觉得所译的文字形象性差或意境不够理想时，他从不勉强定稿，有时找不到更合适的译法宁肯停译，等待“灵感”再生。由于从不动摇修改的意愿，最终总能找到新的突破口，达到自己所追求的目标。他的强项是长期坚持直接用英文写诗，而且与世界诗联有过实际联系，正式发表过自己的英文诗作，有的诗曾得过奖，有的甚至被世界诗协编入美国出版的《2005 年最好的诗人最好的诗》一书。

欧美同学会　李燕朝

Preface

As an editor-in-chief, I had worked in the WRSA (Western Returned Scholars Association) from 1987 till 2009. I had been in charge of the American-returned alumni association to compile and publish the WRSA Journal (later, the title changed to be Chinese Overseas Students with an additional one, namely, the WRSA Bulletin). Since then I had more opportunities to meet Manfield Zhu for reading his more and more manuscripts in different kinds of writings to be published in the journal.

As a visiting scholar, Manfield Zhu had studied at the University of Illinois, Urbana-Champaign, United States of America. He was a professor of English at the Capital University of Economics and Business, China, and a senior translator conferred by the Chinese Translators Organization. He has had more concurrent posts and elected as vice president of American-returned alumni association. He was more concerned about the WRSA alumni service, often wrote some papers to report the American-returned alumni activities; usually, his wrote or translations, either on poetry or on essay or news report would be sent to me firstly.

Manfield Zhu is considered as a versatile alumnus member with a facile imagination. He is good at writing fast and effectively. Sometimes his writing style is humorous a little bit. I have had good memories of his careful consideration of some well-known translators. Once he sharply pointed out their some shortcomings or serious mistakes. For example, in the English version of *A Dream of Red Mansions* translated by Yang Xianyi "watchman's wooden clappers" was mistaken for "frogs' croaking" and that was found 27 years later after the book was published for the first version. For such a long time, even no one had pointed out the wrong translation except Manfield Zhu. The WRSA Bulletin published Manfield Zhu's academic paper to retranslate four metrical poems on Spring, Summer, Autumn and Winter to correct something wrong of the original version of *A Dream of Red Mansions* translated by Mr. and Mrs. Yang. I am envious of his fearless spirit to seek for the truth. As time goes on, with more and more mutually cultural exchanges, he would like to ask me to read and check up his writings.

In 2012, I was trusted to compile his 256 translation of poems from the Chinese ancient period of time to present, almost including all the famous and typical poems which can represent the essence of classic and modern Chinese poetry. As an anthology, the book entitled *Chinese Famous Poetry Translated by Manfield Zhu* which was published in autumn, 2013, and three years later, the Commercial Press International Co., Ltd. published the book again as the second edition in addition of 20 newly-translated poems. Right now the book is still sell well. In 2014, he translated *Complete Collection of Li Yu's Poetry*. I was glad to write a preface to this book. Recently I am told the book is to sell well, and the publishing house will publish more copies to meet more readers' need.

"The more plowing and weeding will have the better crop." Right now Manfield Zhu has completed translating *Complete Collection of Li Qingzhao's Poetry Translated by Manfield Zhu*. He said "it is the most reluctant or timid for me to hand in such a translation manuscript to a publishing house". Because there are too many talented translators who have translated Li Qingzhao's Song poems into English, it is more difficult for any fresh translator to surpass their translation levels. He said if your version had no outstanding features to show to all the readers, it is really unnecessary to publish your manuscripts. Actually the translation manuscripts was completed a year ago, but on purpose, he left them alone, he would like to wait for a new flash idea that would come into his mind and then he could retranslate or revise them again. During a whole year, he has repeatedly revised one poem after another. He often tries to play a role as a native speaker to recite his own translation poem and seeks for English senses. At the same time, he has paid much more attention to researching Li Qingzhao's family and social background. In order to interpret the poetess' inside meaning of her each poem, he made more helpful annotations to some key words or difficult words or expressions. Manfield Zhu takes more careful consideration and more researching time on this book's manuscript than his two published books. Therefore, from his translation annotations, readers can benefit very much for deeply understanding Li Qingzhao's inner world and her poetry's context and rich imagination. He has a strong desire that his translation works will not be just a flower vase in front of our poetess' west window, but like a red candle burning to brighten her mind. And also he hopes his newly-translated works will be like a long corridor to let all the passengers enjoy our poetess' beauty.

Finally I'd like to say that his English translation poems are more like original ones, and that is the characteristic of his English translation. He is very concerned about the feedback or comment from his English teachers and classmates. He will try to know his translation works is really good or not, never self-righteous. If he finds his translation image is poorer or the mood is not so better than original text, he will never reluctantly finalized, and sometimes he cannot find a more appropriate translation, he would rather stop translating but waiting for "inspiration" regeneration. Because his will or perseverance is extremely strong, and ultimately he can always find a new breakthrough, to achieve his ideal goal. His strong point is that he has kept on writing in English directly, and also he always pays attention to the trend from international poets organization which has officially published his English poems, some of which was rewarded by success, and others have been published. And one of his poems was compiled in the book entitled *The Best Poets and the Best Poems of 2005* published in America.

Yanchao Lee,
The Western Returned Scholars Association

自 序

从2015年晚秋到2017年初夏，历时21个月，把李清照遗留下来的所有诗词，凡是有据可查的，都搜集起来了，形成了一本电子版的全集。唯恐网上得来的版本有疏漏，最后确定将1979年人民文学出版社出版的王仲闻先生《李清照集校注》纸版全集为主要依据，敲定了其全部诗词篇目，开始英译；同时参照了多种版本的注释，修正了一些明显的技术性的错误。

在英译的过程中，译者大部分时间都用在了查找、阅读与作品有关的具体时代背景资料上了，同时对李清照一生所经历的具体历史事件做了更深入细致的研读。为英译李清照作品，首先不得不再重温北宋、南宋时期所发生的重要历史事件；不得不顺着李清照的行踪重新阅读她特别熟悉的许许多多的历史典故或轶事。

能否准确无误地把中国古典诗词译成外文？译者从不敢站出来说一句“我行！”。多年来，只是默默地在跟美国英文老师和朋友进行这方面的尝试。译者相信，人类任何语言都是用来交流的，其中任何两种语言之间必然是可以相互理解的。即使中国的诗词曲赋等文学样式有诸多特殊性，仍难阻挡人们进行这种文化交流或翻译的尝试。

在具体翻译李清照诗词实践过程中所遇到的困难，往往不完全在语言文字本身，而在于女词人熟悉的，译者并不太熟悉。这是译者遇到的，也是无法回避的第一大困难。

语言文字方面的困难主要是源于不同语言文字之间的差异性。英译汉语古典诗词，特别是译格律诗，如何体现其平仄、黏对、拗救、对仗、防犯孤平、押平声韵等要求是很棘手的问题。对格律的某些要求，译者不能全做得到，有时甚至是无计可施，因此在很多情况下，只能“求大同，存小异”。对译者来说，最重要的是必须尽最大努力传递好原文的重要信息和意境，不得随意浅化或淡化，不得用散文式的抽象化、概念化的语言取代诗词的形象化语言。必须大体上实现内容和形式的统一、神似貌似，即神貌结合，不如此，便难以让英文读者较好地感受到原文的味道。译者必须力求做到译诗像诗、译出意境、大体押韵、语言形象、自然流畅、节奏感强、易读易解。

英语没有汉语“平、上、去、入”四声的语音体系，但是英汉两种语言的发音仍有很大的可比性。让所英译的诗词按其自身韵律规矩押韵并不难。在这方面，我国译界的泰斗已经做出了示范，为晚辈提供了可贵的理论与技巧。

“他山之石，可以攻玉”。虚心学习、领会、借鉴诗歌翻译大家的经验，如站在巨人的肩头上，后辈人不仅可以增强信心，也可以少走弯路。董仲舒《春秋繁露》首次提出“诗无达诂”的论断，既然诗都没有通达的解释，也不能确切的训诂，那么，诗或诗词曲赋等类似的文学体裁的外文译文就更难求得所谓的标准的译文了。译者更没有这个胆量说自己译得好、译得标准！以前不敢说，今后随着诗词译者队伍的扩大也不敢这样自信地说。不过，没勇气自以为是，却有傻气亮相，敢于把自己的译文拿出来晒晒。希望抛砖引玉，促进讨论，从而能出现更多的译文版本，让译界真正出现百家争鸣、百花齐放的新局面。

通读自己译稿后，想具体说几句《李清照诗词英译全集》译文所涉及的翻译思路。

【I】韵律

以英译李清照《如梦令》“常记溪亭日暮，沉醉不知归路”为例：

I often remember sundown over river pavilion dome,

Being intoxicated so deeply to lose my back way home.

此译文同原文相比：(1)没有漏掉原文的信息。(2)有韵律，读起来自然、流畅、上口。(3)总的字数基本上与原文一致，整首词实现了形式与内容的统一。

【II】对仗

以李清照《乌江》“生当作人杰，死亦为鬼雄”为例：

Alive, as a hero I live my life,

Dead, as a ghost king I died.

英文平均每个单词长度约5个字母，每个字母占位相同，但每个单词占位不尽相同。这种语言文字体系决定了它不太容易形成汉语对联似的语言结构——也就是说，缺乏汉语那种对仗的文字基础。汉诗英译时，只能从概念上、语序上实现对仗，要想在字形字数上完全对仗几乎是不可能的。

李清照《乌江》五言绝句前两句开头的字分别为“生”和“死”，二者“对仗”。两个字均为动词，根据翻译理论与技巧的普通常识，用英语的形容词 Alive 和 Dead 来译汉语“生”和“死”两个动词，恰到好处。

英文诗押韵的模式，常见的有 A-A-B-B、A-B-A-B 或 A-A-B-A（详见 *The Norton Anthology of Poetry* 5th Edition）。这首五言绝句译文押韵的模式与地道的英文诗的韵律基本是吻合的。

中国古代魏晋以后产生过一种特讲究对仗的文体——骈体文，南北朝时达到了全盛时期。其主要特点是以四六句式为主，讲究对仗，句式两两相对。英文从没有过这样的语文发展历史阶段。英文不以对仗或并列、排比式的语言结构见长。因此，译者进行翻译实践时必须有意识的“扬长避短”。在好多情况下，中文的并列结构也可以译成偏正结构、主谓结构。

例如，李清照《一剪梅·红藕香残玉簟秋》下半阕中：

“一种相思，两处闲愁。”

“才下眉头，却上心头。”

这类对比很明显的词语或句结，也完全可以用英文偏正结构或句结来译。

“There’s one kind of lovesickness,

Coming from two places with sadness.”

“Just falling down from my eyebrows,

Into my heart with sorrows. ”

【III】韵脚的选择

只要充分利用中英两种语言中可比性较强的因素，求得译文韵律的和谐美是有潜力的。译者尽量选择了音域宽阔的开口长元音或双元音为尾韵，如，[ɑː] [əː] [iː] [ɔː] [aɪ] [eɪ] [aʊ] [əʊ]；少用浊辅音 [v] [z] [ʒ] [dʒ]；根据情况使用鼻音 [m] [n] [ŋ] [l]、清辅音 [t] [k] 等为收尾音。需要特别强调的是不论在任何情况下都不得为了凑韵而害义，不得为了凑韵而造成信息的缺失。

试将李清照《声声慢》[①] 中这几行与英译做一比较：

三杯两盏淡酒，

怎敌他、晓来风急？

雁过也，

正伤心，

却是旧时相识。

Two or three cups of soft wine,

Could stop dawn wind in cry?

The flying wild geese in a line,

As my old friends in the sky,

Being sad, I'm heartbroken with a sigh.

英译五行的收尾词，分别为 wine、cry、line、sky、sigh, 其中，第一、三、五行押韵，韵脚为 [aɪn]——开口双元音，读起来很上口，很响亮。第二、四行收尾音 [aɪ] 与第一、三、五行的韵脚差别不大，所以，从总体来说，这几行诗词音响效果不错。

【Ⅳ】“叠字”或重复字词问题

如何英译李清照《声声慢》里的“寻寻觅觅，冷冷清清，凄凄惨惨戚戚”这类叠字成堆的词组历来有争议。英语中，虽然也有“long, long ago”“very, very good”等“叠字”用法，但同汉语“叠字”出现的频率相比是微不足道的。如果模仿汉语模式，将此用法扩大到更多的不同词性的词汇上，那么，以英语为母语的读者会觉得不习惯，会给人故弄玄虚的感觉。通常，英语并不以这类重复的方式来加强语气。因此，译者若只求此“形似”往往收不到主观预想的效果。

英译这类由“叠字”或并列词组组成的句结时，首先要从英文语法、语义两大方面，也就是从总体上把握其内容和结构的关系。如果不能根据默默控制文字之间内在关系的语法结构或逻辑思维来判定词与词之间的关系，译者就要按英语结构要求，酌情填补文字的施主，即主语，不如此就只能译成洋泾浜式的英语。为此，译者就必须有意识地把这类并列结构的词组，变通为英语语法可接受的结构。不然，按照“古道西风瘦马”“小桥流水人家”这类无谓语动词的诗句模式来英译会是很不地道的。

现将“寻寻觅觅，冷冷清清，凄凄惨惨戚戚”试译如下：

I am to seek, seek and look for what I think,

I feel cold, lonely, so sad and so tragic,

To be sorrowful, unhappy and lovesick.

这里译者根据语法或逻辑的基本要求酌情填补必要的主语；也重复使用了有关词汇并通过计算机将此英译文还原成中文，达到了预想的结果。

李清照《声声慢》这首词是她晚年所作，她遭遇国破家亡、丈夫去世，那时她独自一人在异乡漂泊，流离失所，怀念往昔的生活。回忆增加她对现实苦楚的感受，回忆和现实的悲伤也重叠了，她反复用叠字表达感受也成了这首词的独特韵味。叠字的连贯使用，细微地传达出了女词人的感伤心境。千古之下，读之仍催人泪下。

英译时熟悉女词人写此词时的具体背景是非常重要的，不可只咬文嚼字。译者在英译李清照诗词全集之前，曾先后出版过《中国历代诗词英译集锦》《李煜诗词英译全集》《赵朴初咏茶诗集》，曾直接得到过商务印书馆国际有限公司、中国外文出版发行事业局朝华出版社等行家里手的点拨。长期以来，大翻译家都是有选择地翻译她有代表性的诗词，而译者显得有点“狂妄”，非要全译，这主要是想为中外关心研究李清照作品的志士仁人提供较详尽的资料性读物。更多的资料会有助于专家、学者、教授们更客观、更准确地认识李清照、解读李清照。同时也是出于译者对李清照的偏爱与崇拜。

2016年秋商务印书馆国际有限公司再版了我的译作《中国历代诗词英译集锦》，2017年6月出版我的《李煜诗词英译全集》，此书刚出版两个月就加印，并挤进了畅销的行列，这在很大程度上，等于进一步肯定了我的译文，因而也增强了我英译李清照所有诗词的决心和信心。译者希望自己少空发译论，多出译作，继续为“中国文化走向世界——影响人类未来”的伟大文化工程添砖加瓦。

在翻译的过程中，喜忧参半，想译得简练、达意、韵美又不得随意增减或变通原文的信息，谈何容易！翻译也是充满遗憾的事情。译了几百首诗词之后，回过头来再看自己的译文往往会有诸多不满意之处。这类的遗憾可能会折磨自己一生，这是普通读者未必都能意识得到的。

通过自己翻译的具体实践深深感到，翻译是学好一门外语、提高自己外语表达能力的有效手段，不可低估。对个人来说，英译每一首古典诗词同时也是重温一段历史、重新深入学习、欣赏历史故事的极好机会。英译的最大受益者是译者本人。希望这本译作也有好运，有机会参与中西文化交流，一如自己曾经英译过的《赵朴初咏茶诗集》（此书已得到中国社科院有关负责人通知，今年亦将再版）——曾作为中国社会科学院赠送给“第七届国际二宫尊德[②]思想学会大会”的礼品（2016年8月24日至25日在日本东京明治大学召开）。

时下恰巧是译者的《李煜诗词英译全集》出版问世的时候，为自己的新译作写序言，内心世界充满了感激之情。饮水思源，首先要感谢出版社笔友们的非常精益求精、非常严谨的工作作风，感谢他（她）们为出好我的书替我吃了太多辛苦。

借此机会，我不能不特别感谢英国伦敦诗歌出版社（驻纽约办事处）尼格尔·希拉里对我诗作的关注和鼓励。希拉里曾于2006年2月15日特意发来电子邮件高度评价被美国收编出版过的朱曼华英文诗作——“最近，令人愉快的是我读到了你已经在美国出版的诗歌[③]，我祝贺你的力作问世；并且我认为你的独特的才华、与众不同的视角得到国际社会的赞誉也是顺理成章的。”希拉里的点评极大地鼓舞了我用英文写诗、译诗的勇气和决心。从此，我更感到直接参与国际文化交流的伟大意义和可能性。

尼格尔·希拉里这封约稿信使我直接听到了以英语为母语的西方朋友对自己英文诗作或译作的反馈，这个信息极大地激发了我写译的热情，的确令人终生难忘！

最后但并非最不值得记载。我谢世的妻子曾长期为我解读过李清照等杰出女词人的作品，她曾一直是我最好的家庭教师。在近两年的时间里，她的倩影一直陪伴我、鼓励我、支持我，似乎仍在一个一个具体回答我所遇到的具体问题。

【译注】

① 本书译者于2013年秋由商务印书馆国际有限公司出版的《中国历代诗词英译集锦》曾选译过这首《声声慢》，其译文与此译文略有变动。

② 二宫尊德（Ninomiya Sontoku，1787—1856），日本江户后期政家，名金次郎，相模国人。出身于农家，一生致力于村藩的改革和复兴，以农村实践家著称。对明治时的资本主义发展有很大影响。著有《报德记》《报德外记》，后刊有《二宫尊德全集》全三十六卷。

③ 这里指的是朱曼华直接用英文写的诗——（1）《伞》Umbrella/Beaty Shadow；（2）《清西陵的黄昏》Emperor Tomb at Dusk；（3）《河畔》Along the Riverside。这三首诗于2005年分别被收编在美国三本诗歌选集中，即（1）Eternal Portraits《永恒的彩绘》，（2）The International Who's Who in Poetry Anthology《国际诗歌名人录》，（3）The Best Poets and the Best Poems of 2005《2005年最好的诗人最好的诗》。

朱曼华于太湖滨湖区

Translator's Preamble

From late autumn 2015 to early summer 2017, which lasted 21 months, all the general classic poems and Song poems (Ci poems) left by Li Qingzhao, all well documented, were collected and formed an electronic version of the Complete Poetic Works. Considering the version of the Internet might have omissions, the translator finally determined to take *Complete Collection of Li Qingzhao's Poetry Translated by Manfield Zhu* proofread by Wang Zhongwen as a formal copy version, which was once published by the People's Literature Publishing House in 1979. The translator took the version proofread by Mr. Wang as the Chinese original text to be translated in English and also based on various versions with annotations written by different proofreaders, and at the same time, Translator Manfield Zhu corrected some obvious technical errors among different versions.

In the process of translation, the translator spent much more time in reading more and more reference materials or works related to the background of some Song poems written by Li Qingzhao whose life was experienced by the specific historical events on which the translator made much deep and meticulous research. In order to translate Li Qingzhao's works, first of all, it is necessary to review what happened to the Northern Song Dynasty or to the Southern Song Dynasty; it is still necessary to think hard about some important historical events; the translator had to follow Li Qingzhao's whereabouts to read many historical allusions or anecdotes she had known very well.

Is it possible to translate Chinese classical poetry into foreign language accurately? The translator did not dare to stand up and say "I do!". For many years, I've just kept in silence but often to exchange with my English teachers and friends in the United States in this attempt. I believe that any language of mankind can be used to communicate, and any two languages must be mutually understood. Even if the Chinese poetry or the other literary poetic works in different styles are with a lot of particularity, nothing can stop people to carry out mutually cultural exchange or translation attempt.

In the course of the specific translation practice, the difficulties encountered are often not entirely in the language itself, and that often came from what the translator was not familiar with the poetess' experience. All the translators could not escape from such difficulties.

Usually, the translation difficulty is mainly due to the differences between different languages in structure and grammar. As for English translation of classical Chinese poetry, especially the translation of metrical poetry, how to translate the Chinese tonal system or the complicated metrical rules or rhythm is quite a difficult problem. There is no way to suit some requirements of the metonymy. It is almost impossible to do well. In many cases, I will only go in for "seeking something similar in general but trying to decrease some differences". The most important thing is to try my best to convey the important information and mood of the original text. I should not be free to lighten or dilute the original text essence. I should not translate in the prose-writing way to make an abstract explanation or just to use the conceptual words or expressions to replace the visual language of poetry. In general I have to achieve the unity of both content and form, and the translated poem should be still like a true poem both in inside meaning and in outside appearance. Otherwise, it is difficult for English readers to better feel the taste of the original poem. The translator must strive to make his translated poem like a true poem, which should be with several Chinese poetic factors, such as harmonious rhyme, vivid expression, natural smooth sequence, strong sense of rhythm, easy to read and easy to understand.

English is with no Chinese four-tonal system, but the English and Chinese pronunciation is still with very large comparability. It is not difficult to let the English translated poem in rhyming according to its own rhythm rules. In this regard, China's great translation masters have made a demonstration for the younger generation to provide a valuable theory and skills.

As a Chinese saying goes, "Taking other mountain's stone, you can grind your own jade". Learning from the experience of poetry translation is like someone standing on a giant's shoulders, the younger generation can not only enhance the confidence, but also make less detours. An ancient Chinese scholar Dong Zhongshu in his works entitled *Bright Dewdrops in Spring and Autumn Dynasty* for the first time put forward a point that "poetry is with no absolutely right explanation". Since poetry is neither to interpret accessibly nor to make exegeses, then, poetry or Song-poetry and other similar literary genre's foreign language translation is even more difficult to understand completely. So there must be no key to answer the so-called standard translation question. The translator did not have the courage to say that my version is translated well enough to reach the translation standard! I did not dare to say so. In the near future with the expansion of the poetry translator team, I will be more afraid to say so confidently. However, with no courage to bragging, I am in a silly debut, I dare to take my own translation under the sun. Hope to initiate pen pals to provoke controversy, which may make more perfect versions so that the community really could create more new translation in new situation, that is, a hundred schools of translation thought contend as if a hundred flowers were blooming lively.

After reading my own translation, I would like to specifically say a few words. Translating *Complete Collection of Li Qingzhao's Poetry Translated by Manfield Zhu* from Chinese into English left me several flash points in my mind.

[I] The rhyme

Firstly, let me take the English translation of Ci poetess, Li Qingzhao's *Like a Dream Verse* as an example.

(The original text)

《如梦令》

"常记溪亭日暮，沉醉不知归路。"

(The English translation)

I often remember sundown over river pavilion dome,

Being intoxicated so deeply to lose my back way home.

Compared with the original text: (1) the English translation did not miss any of the original information; (2) with rhythm to read naturally smooth, very catchy; (3) the total number of sentences, the number of words are basically the same with the original, the whole Song poems or lyrics achieve the unity of form and content.

[II] The distich

(Two adjacent sentences in a poem like a couplet symmetry)

(The original text)

《乌江》

“生当作人杰，死亦为鬼雄。”

Alive, as a hero I live my life,

Dead, as a ghost king I died.

The average length of each English word is about 5 letters, each letter occupies the same space, but each word occupies different space. This language system determines that it is not easy to form the language structure of Chinese couplet-like structure, that is, English is in shortage of Chinese language's distich or symmetry. The English translation of Chinese poetry only could achieve the distich-symmetry in concept or meaning or word order. It is almost impossible to fully achieve the couple-like distich (symmetry in word-to-word, phrase-to-phrase or sentence-to-sentence in poetic structure so as to achieve the literary symmetry both in content and form, especially in sound of poetry) .

In Li Qingzhao's *Wujiang River* (Chinese metrical 5-character poem), it is not difficult to find that the couplet-distich structure, such as "Alive is contrasted to dead; Male hero is contrasted to ghost king."

Even from the English translation a reader can see that the so-called Chinese couplet-like poetic structure—distich also can be translated to such a structure in English sometimes, so the couplet-like distich can be expressed not only just in a single word-to-word way, phrase-to-phrase way, but also in a sentence-to-sentence way, which is considered as a poetry-writing attractively expressive skill.

The English common rhyming pattern is like this: AABB, ABAB or AABA (see *The Norton Anthology of Poetry* 5th Edition). The English translation of rhyme pattern is basically consistent with the above-mentioned Chinese quatrain rhyme pattern. That is to say, the English translation is not completely impossible to simulate the original text both in content and in form.

During the later Wei and Jin dynasties, China, a special literary style of writing appeared, which is called the Pianti-style prose (parallel prose), placing emphas is on couplet-distich and reaching its heyday in the Northern and Southern Dynasties. Its main feature is of four or six sentence-distich structure. English has never had such a language development history. English is not strong in linguistic couplet-distich or symmetry. Therefore, the translator to carry out translation practice must be conscious of the "strong point and weak point". In many cases, the Chinese side-by-side structure or couplet-distich symmetric structure ought to be translated into a subject-predicate structure as the non-symmetric.

For example, in the last half part of Li Qingzhao's *A Blooming plum*, there are two sentences, including four symmetric 4-character phrases as follows:

"一种相思，两处闲愁。"

"才下眉头，却上心头。"

This type of couplet-ditich sentence also can be translated into non-symmetric structure in English.

"There's one kind of lovesickness,

Coming from two places with sadness."

"Just falling down from my eyebrows,

Into my heart with sorrows."

[III] The rhyme choice

We should make full use of the comparatively powerful factors in the Chinese and English languages, and it is possible to obtain the harmonious beauty of the rhythm of the translation. The translator can try to select the wide range of long vowels or double vowels for the end of the rhyme, such as [ɑ:] [ə:] [i:] [ɔ:] [aɪ] [eɪ] [aʊ] [əʊ] and nasal sound [m] [n] [ŋ] [l] or clear consonants [t] [k] and so on for the ending of the sound, but less use the sounds such as [v] [s] [z] [ʒ] [dʒ] which are not clearly pleasant to the human sense. It needs to be emphasized particularly that in any case the translator shall not sacrifice the inside meaning and information in order to make a rhyme.

Let me make a comparison between Li Qingzhao's following translation poetic lines and the original text quoted from *Sounds Go Slow*:

三杯两盏淡酒，
怎敌他、晓来风急？
雁过也，
正伤心，
却是旧时相识。

Two or three cups of soft wine,
Could stop dawn wind in cry?
The flying wild geese in a line,
As my old friends in the sky,
Being sad, I'm heartbroken with a sigh.

The English translation's five characters at the end of each sentence respectively are wine, cry, line, sky, and sigh, whose rhyme belonging to "A-B-A-B-A"rhyming pattern of [aɪn]-[aɪ]-[aɪn]-[aɪ]-[aɪn]—open double vowel, being very clear, catchy. The second and the fourth sentence is at the end by pronounciation [aɪ] respectively, and the first, third and fifth line are to rhyme in rhyme[aɪn] very harmoniously, so in general, this poetry's sound is in good effect.

[IV] The "stacked word" or the word repetition

How to translate Li Qingzhao's Song-poem, *Sounds Go Slow* with plenty of "stacked word" has always been controversial. In English, although there are "long, long ago" "very, very good" and other "stacked word" seemed to be popular, still the frequency of Chinese "stacked word" is much higher than that of English. However, the less "word repetition" in English is not the reason to be negligible. If imitating the Chinese model, this usage will be extended to more different parts of the word, then the English-speaking readers will not feel natural and comfortable. It will give them mysterious impression. Often, English does not strengthen the tone in such a repetitive way.

In this context, we must first grasp the relationship between the content and the structure from the two aspects of English grammar and semantics. If the inherent relationship between one word and the other was impossible to make sure according to the structure or logic about the text, the translator should fill the subject word, a pronoun or a noun which would control each word of the sentence. Otherwise, if no subject is used to control a series of words or expressions, then there must be something wrong, and that would not be an idiomatic sentence structure in English. To this end, the translator must consciously change this kind of juxtaposed structure of the phrase into the acceptable structure of English grammar. Otherwise, in accordance with the poem's two lines—"Ancient road westerly wind thin horse" "Little bridge flowing water people home", the verb-less sentences are without any linking verb, which will not be okay both in grammar and in meaning, and that's not a correct English translation.

Now let me have a try to translate poetess Li Qingzhao's *Sounds Go Slow* full of word-repetition structures like this:

I am to seek, seek and look for what I think,

I feel cold, lonely, so sad and so tragic,

To be sorrowful, unhappy and lovesick.

It's getting abruptly warm,still cold,

Keeping fit for me is difficult.

In Chinese poetry, some subjects are often omitted but in English sometimes it is necessary for the translator to add some subject so as to make up complete sentences. In the above translation, without "I feel" , then the whole poem will not be okay in grammar. If "seek" is without "to", then the first whole sentence will not be okay, too. Therefore, the translator must learn how to use the morphological way to express the Chinese inside meaning.

Li Qingzhao wrote the *Sounds Go Slow* at her age of later years when she suffered both a national death and her husband's death. Then she was alone in some southern cities of China, wandering, being displaced, recalling her past life. Her early memories increased her feelings of pain. And the reality of sadness overlapped the pain that she was repeatedly used to express in her Song-poems, which became her Song-poem's unique charm. She was good at using the "stacked word" to transmit her coherent subtle and sentimental mood. A thousand years later, reading her Song-poetry still excites more and more people shedding.

It is extremely necessary for the translator to be familiar with the poetess' detailed background and some allusions or literary quotations and anecdotes she knew very well. It was very helpful for everyone to understand her special background with her rich knowledge. As a poetess, she was often immersed in social practice and Chinese history. As a translator, it may not be a good idea just to translate her works in word-to-word way.

Before translating *Complete Collection of Li Qingzhao's Poetry Translated by Manfield Zhu*, I published other works entitled *Chinese Famous Poetry Translated by Manfield Zhu*, *Complete Collection of Li Yu's Poetry*, *Zhao Puchu's Anthology of the Tea Culture*. I directly obtained more guidance from the Commercial Press International Co.,Ltd., from the National Foreign Language Bureau of China's publishing house and their editorial experts. For a long time, the great translators have chosen to translate the poetess' representative poems selectively, but this time, the translator is a bit arrogant, and I am determined to translate her complete poetic works altogether. my main reason is to provide a more detailed description and information for the Chinese scholars and students as well as all the fans of the poetess. More and more Chinese young people are interested in studying Li Qingzhao's works with rich annotations. So that experts, scholars and professors will have more information, helping them have more objective and more accurate understanding of Li Qingzhao. For a long long time, the translator has been fond and respectful of Li Qingzhao's poetic works.

In the autumn of 2016, the Commercial Press International Co., Ltd. reprinted my translation works *Chinese Famous Poetry Translated by Manfield Zhu*, which further confirmed my faithful translation, strengthened my determination and confidence to translate all the poems and Ci lyrics of Li Qingzhao. I hope I will be less to talk about translation theory but do more translation works, so as to continue my goal to "let Chinese culture spread over the world to influence the human future". Let me try to add more building bricks for the great cultural engineering.

In the process of translation, I am happy a half and sad a half. I would like to make my translation concise, meaningful, rhythmical and not free to increase or decrease the original text information, but easier said than done! Translation is also full of regrets. After translation of hundreds of poems, coming back to see my own translation, I have a lot of dissatisfactions. This kind of regret may torture my whole life.

Through my own translation of the specific practice, I deeply feel that translation is an effective means to learn a foreign language, to improve my ability to master a foreign language, and that can not be underestimated. For the individual, the English translation of each classical poetry means re-studying a period of history, so as a translator, he should appreciate the great opportunity to review the historical stories. The greatest beneficiary of the English translation is the translator himself. I hope that this translation is also a good luck, a unique opportunity to participate in the exchange of Chinese and Western cultures, as my own English translation of the *Zhao Puchu's Anthology of the Tea Culture was* once used as a gift of the Chinese Academy of Social Sciences presented to the "The seventh International Ninomiya Sontoku ethics society symposium" (August 24 to 25, 2016, Tokyo, Japan).

Nowadays, when my English translation version of *Complete Collection of Li Yu's Poetry* is formally published, I write a preface to my own newly-translated version of *Complete Collection of Li Qingzhao's Poetry Translated by Manfield Zhu*, my heart and mind are full of gratitude. Drinking water needs thinking its source. First of all, I'd like to thank my faithful pen pals for their very good, very rigorous hard-working style, thank editors for their careful consideration of my new translation version.

I'd like to take this opportunity to extend my heartfelt thanks to Nigel Hillary Publisher, Poetry Division Noble House U.K., who wrote to me directly to praise my poems being compiled and published in America; at the same time I was invited to write a new English poem for Poetry Division Noble House U.K.. Nowadays still I feel happy to read the letter, something like this: "Recently, I had the pleasure of reading the poetry that you have had published in the United States. I congratulate you on this grand endeavour, and propose to you that your singular talent and vision deserves appropriate international recognition as well." "For this reason, I have posted this letter to request your permission to include one of your favourite poems in Songs of Honour - a new poetry edition that is being distributed worldwide by Noble House... a collection of poetry that is perhaps unlike any you have ever seen... one where each poem is featured on its own page, and one whose quality is reminiscent of the finest 19th century antique poetry books." (15 February, 2006)

Such an authoritive publisher's praise and encouragement promoted my writing or translating poems in English. Since then I've felt more pleasant to join the international cultural exchanges and I am sure I will do much better.

As a new pen pal, Nigel Hillary let me be sure of my own ability to write or to translate in Englsh. Since then I have kept enthusiastic in writing and translating more and more poems. So I can never forget such an English pen pal.

Last but not least worthy to mention. I have long tears of my wife who had a long time for me to interpret Li Qingzhao and other outstanding works of women. She was my best tutor. In the past two years, her shadows still have been with me, encouraged me, supported me. It seems that she is still answering my questions , one by one, which I encountered in translating.

Manfield Zhu

目 录

卷二　诗
Part Two Poems

附　录

后　记

卷一　词

Part One Ci Poems

南歌子

天上星河转，
人间帘幕垂。
凉生枕簟泪痕滋。
起解罗衣聊问、夜何其①？

翠贴莲蓬小，
金销藕叶稀。
旧时天气旧时衣，
只有情怀、不似旧家时。

The South Palace Song

The Milky Way and stars turn around heaven,
Hanging down the human world is the screen.
The cold makes tears fall on the bed and pillow.
Putting off my silk skirt, I'd like to know where tonight is to go?

Lotus small seedpods like the emerald,
Lotus roots grow up, green leaves turn yellow.
The old weather is unchangeable as the old gown.
Only my mind has no old style to follow.

【译注】

①夜何其（jī）：夜到几更了。语出《诗经·小雅·庭燎》："夜如何其？夜未央。"其：表示疑问的语气词。

转调满庭芳[①]（版本一）

芳草池塘，绿阴庭院，
晚晴寒透窗纱。
□□金鏁[②]，管是客来唦[③]。
寂寞尊前席上，惟□□海角天涯[④]。
能留否？酴醾[⑤]落尽，犹赖有□□。

当年曾胜赏，生香熏袖，活火分茶。
□□龙骄马，流水轻车。
不怕风狂雨骤，恰才称，煮酒残（笺）花[⑥]。
如今也，不成怀抱，得似旧时那？

Homology Variant of Courtyard Full of Fragrance

At the pond spring fragrant grasses grow,
The courtyard shrouded by green shadow,
The setting sun got through my screen.
The gold lock (might be open),
I guessed a guest might come in.
Before wine cups upon dining-table, I sat lonely,
As if feeling far away from my remote country.
What I loved would still remain?
All of spring rose blossoms faded away,
There're still something flowery.

In those years long,
My homeland scenery was spreading on,
Spices made my sleeves fragrant smell,
Boiling water made tea to share with my pal.
The capital street was like a dancing dragon,
The horse-driven carts like current fast ran.
I would fear no storm,
Boiling wine exactly urged my poem.
Nowadays no great ambitions stay,
As the same as my past heyday.

【译注】

①“转调满庭芳”为“满庭芳”之变调，词的格律或平仄有变化。“满庭芳”因唐代吴融“满庭芳草易黄昏”诗句而得名。亦作《锁阳台》《满庭霜》《潇湘夜雨》。

【版本一】见于人民文学出版社《李清照集校注》阙字版（阙同缺）；

【版本二】见于《乐府雅词》；

【版本三】见于清代流传补字版。

②金鏁（suǒ）：金锁。

③管是：必定是；多半是。唦（shā）：助词，用在句末表示揣度、停顿或祈使的语气，大致相当于“吧（ba）”“嘛（ma）”。

④海角天涯：泛指遥远的地方。这里借指北宋国都沦陷后的故国大好河山。

⑤酴醾（tú mí）：这里指花名，属蔷薇科落叶小灌木，暮春时开花，有香气。也作“酴醿”。陆游有《东阳观酴醿》诗：福州正月把离杯，已见酴醿压架开。

⑥残花：《四印斋本·漱玉词》本记作“笺花”。笺花，暗指如花似锦的美诗。

转调满庭芳
（版本二）

芳草池塘，绿阴庭院，
晚晴寒透窗纱。
谁开金鏁，管是客来吵。
寂寞尊前席上，春归去海角天涯。
能留否？酴醾落尽，犹赖有残葩。

当年曾胜赏①，生香熏袖，活火分茶。
尽如龙骄马，流水轻车②。
不怕风狂雨骤，恰才称，煮酒残（笺）花。
如今也，不成怀抱，得似旧时那？

【译注】

①胜赏：对故土美景赏心悦目。

②尽如龙骄马，流水轻车：作者忆起当年常出游繁华闹市，车水马龙，感慨万千，更激起了对丈夫南渡以后逃走行径的愤慨，曾奋笔疾书，写下了她那千古绝句——“生当作人杰，死亦为鬼雄。至今思项羽，不肯过江东。”

Homology Variant of Courtyard Full of Fragrance

At the pond spring fragrant grasses grow,
The courtyard shrouded by green shadow,
The setting sun got through my screen.
Who might have the locked door open?
I guessed a guest might come in.
Before wine cups upon dining-table, I sat lonely,
As if feeling far away from my remote country.
What I loved would still stay?
Residual flowers were still wonderful,
All the spring rose blossoms faded away.

In those years long,
My homeland scenery was spreading on,
Spices made my sleeves fragrant smell,
Boiling water made tea to share with my pal.
The best is the capital street like a dancing dragon,
The horse-driven carts like current fast ran.
I would fear no storm,
Boiling wine exactly urged my poem.
Nowadays no great ambitions stay,
As the same as my past heyday.

转调满庭芳
（版本三）

芳草池塘，绿阴庭院，
晚晴寒透窗纱。
玉钩金锁[1]，管是客来吵。
寂寞尊前席上，唯愁海角天涯。
能留否？酴醾落尽，犹赖有梨花[2]。

当年曾胜赏[3]，生香熏袖，活火分茶。
极目（犹）龙骄马[4]，流水轻车。
不怕风狂雨骤，恰才称，煮酒笺花。
如今也，不成怀抱，得似旧时那[5]？

【译注】

①玉钩金锁：弯弯的月牙点亮夜空，门上的金锁静静的低垂。

②梨花：为后代版本补字。

③胜赏：风流赏会。

④极目（犹）龙骄马：按格律，此句多一个字，犹字可去掉。

⑤得似旧时那：不敢想起那些美好的时光。得似那：哪得似。那是语助词。

Homology Variant of Courtyard Full of Fragrance

At the pond spring fragrant grasses grow,
The courtyard shrouded by green shadow,
The setting sun got through my screen.
The lock hung of gate, the moon like a bow in the heaven,
I guessed a guest might come in.
Before wine cups upon dining-table, I sat lonely,
As if feeling far away from my remote country.
What I loved would still remain?
All of spring rose blossoms faded away,
Just pear blossoms still blooming again?

In those years long,
My homeland scenery was spreading on,
Spices made my sleeves fragrant smell,
Boiling water made tea to share with my pal.
My best joy was the capital street like a dancing dragon,
The horse-driven carts like current fast ran.
I would fear no storm,
Boiling wine exactly urged my poem.
Nowadays I have no ambitious stay,
As the same as my past heyday.

渔家傲[1]

雪里已知春信[2]至，
寒梅点缀琼枝腻[3]。
香脸半开娇旖旎[4]，
当庭际，玉人[5]浴出新妆洗。

造化[6]可能偏有意，
故教明月玲珑[7]地。
共赏金尊沈绿蚁[8]，
莫辞醉，此花不与群花比。

Fisherman Pride

The snow knows the vernal arrival,
The cold plum blossom decorates twigs to be beautiful.
All the blossom in half bloom look gentle in charm,
Like a makeup madam from her bathroom.

The creator might be on purpose in mind to make the moon bright,
And show such a seeing sight.
Now share gold cups of wine,
Then go on in a tipsy mind,
For no other group of flowers more beautiful than the plum blossom.

【译注】

①渔家傲：词牌名。因晏殊词有“神仙一曲渔家傲”句。

②春信：春天消息。

③点缀：装饰衬托。琼枝：此指梅枝着雪，白如玉枝。腻：梅枝着雪后变得粗肥。

④香脸：此处比拟半开着的散发芳香的梅花。旖旎（yǐ nǐ）：柔和美好的样子。

⑤玉人：美人。这里喻指梅花。

⑥造化：天地，大自然。

⑦玲珑：明彻貌。

⑧尊：同“樽”。金尊，酒杯。沈：同“沉”。绿蚁：古代为酒的代称。

如梦令

昨夜雨疏风骤，
浓睡不消残酒，
试问卷帘人，
却道海棠依旧。
知否？知否？
应是绿肥红瘦。

Like a Dream Verse

Last night it drizzled and suddenly windy,
A deep sleep later, still I was tipsy,
Opening the roller blind, the maid told so:
“The crabapple trees bloom as usual.”
You know? You know?
The green is more, the red few.

如梦令

常记溪亭日暮，
沉醉不知归路。
兴尽晚回舟，
误入藕花深处。
争渡，争渡，
惊起一滩鸥鹭。

Like a Dream Verse

I often remember sundown over river pavilion
dome,
Being intoxicated so deeply to lose my back
way home.
Full enjoy later, returning on boat,
To take a wrong road where lotuses grow.
Paddle, paddle!
Gulls on a beach suddenly fly in a row.

多丽
咏白菊

小楼寒，夜长帘幕低垂。
恨萧萧、无情风雨，夜来揉损琼肌①。
也不似、贵妃醉脸，也不似、孙寿②愁眉。
韩令③偷香，徐娘④傅粉，莫将比拟未新奇。
细看取，屈平陶令⑤，风韵正相宜。
微风起，清芬酝藉⑥，不减酴醿⑦。

渐秋阑、雪清玉瘦，向人无限依依。
似愁凝、汉皋解佩⑧，似泪洒、纨扇题诗⑨。
朗月清风，浓烟暗雨，天教憔悴度芳姿。
纵爱惜，不知从此，留得几多时。
人情好，何须更忆，泽畔东篱。

【译注】

①琼肌：指花瓣像玉一般的白菊。

②孙寿：东汉梁冀之妻，色美而善为妖态，她画的眉，长而曲折，时号"愁眉"（见《后汉书·梁冀传》）。

③韩令：指晋人韩寿。韩寿本是贾充的掾吏，被贾充女贾午看中，韩逾墙与午私通，午以

Much Beautiful
Ode to White Chrysanthemum

It's my cold small pavilion,
Long night rolled down the curtain.
I hated the pitiless pattering wind with rain,
The nightmare made jade-like petals broken.
Such white flowers were unlike Yang Guifei's ①
look,
Unlike Sunshou's ② sad brows painted in
black.
I could imagine a romantic anecdote.
Gentleman Han Shou received a royal
princess' gift.
Lady Xu ③ transferred the royal makeup
powder,
Don't say such a romantic allusion as a
wonder,
Carefully I look at the elegant chrysanthemum,
Being in Qu Yuan's or Tao Qian's ④ style or
rhyme.
The breeze is to whistle,
Everywhere was full of fragrant smell,
Not less than wild roses tasteful.

It's gradually late autumn,
With snow-white chrysanthemum,
She is endlessly reluctant to leave for man.
As if being in deep sorrow to release her love
jewel,

Shedding tears to recite a fan-poem⑤ well.
The moon is bright with the clear wind in the heaven,
Where the fog is thick with the rain,
The sky let the fragrant flowers haggard again.
Though I love you, chrysanthemum,
I don't know how long you will keep in bloom.
The human love is perfect,
There's no need to recall the poet,
Once writing a swamp-side fence east.

晋武帝赐贾充的奇香赠韩寿，贾充发觉后即以女嫁韩。

④徐娘：指梁元帝的妃子徐昭佩。《南史·梁元帝徐妃传》有徐妃傅粉"为半面妆"之典故，激怒了元帝。

⑤屈平陶令：屈原名平，陶渊明（潜）曾任彭泽令。

⑥酝藉（yùn jiè）：宽和有涵容。形容人风雅潇洒，才华横溢。也形容文章诗画意趣飘逸含蓄。

⑦酴醿（tú mí）：即荼蘼，花名，花黄如酒，开于春末。

⑧汉皋（gāo）：山名。佩：古人衣带上的玉饰。

⑨纨（wán）扇题诗：指班婕妤题诗团扇以抒发被弃的幽怨。

【Annotation】

① Yang Guifei: Yang Yuhuan (719~756), the most beautiful concubine of Emperor Li Longji, Tang Dynasty, China.

② Sunshou: She was a wife of Great General Liang Ji, the East Han Dynasty, China.

③ Lady Xu: refers to Xu Zhaopei who was a romantic concubine of Emperor Xiao Yi (508~555), the Liang Dynasty, China.

④ Qu Yuan（340BC ~ 278 BC）and Tao Qian (365 ? ~ 427) : ancient great poets of China.

⑤ fan-poem: written by Banjieyu（48 BC~2AD）, an ancient writer, poetess and selected to be one of concubines of Emperor Liu Ao, Han Dynasty, China.

菩萨蛮

风柔日薄春犹早，
夹衫乍著心情好。
睡起觉微寒，
梅花鬓上残。

故乡何处是，
忘了除非醉。
沉水①卧时烧，
香消酒未消。

Beautiful and Long-Haired Dancers

The early spring's full of mild breeze and sunshine,
The cotton gown's to warm my happy mind.
Waking up later, I felt coldish,
My hair-inserted's plum blossom is not fresh.

Where is my hometown?
Unless drunk, I will not forget it down.
I slept, the fragrant wood burnt,
While the smell disappearing,
I am still in a drunk state.

【译注】

①沉水：即沉香，一种贵重的熏香。

菩萨蛮

归鸿声断残云碧，
背窗雪落炉烟直。
烛底凤钗明，
钗头人胜轻。

角声催晓漏，
曙色回牛斗[①]。
春意看花难，
西风留旧寒。

Beautiful and Long-Haired Dancers

The wild geese call, gradually vanishing in the blue sky,
Outside the window, snow falls as smoke rising up high.
The phoenix hair-pin is bright under the candle light,
The lovely pin let the pretty girl still a highlight.

As the horn-bugle calling the ancient timer,
The dawn light shines over the Altair and Big Dipper.
It is melancholy to look at the spring flowers,
The west wind is reluctant to leave for the winter.`

【译注】

①牛斗：星宿名，牛宿和斗宿。

浣溪沙

莫许杯深琥珀浓①，
未成沉醉意先融。
疏钟②已应晚来风。

瑞脑③香消魂梦断，
辟寒金小髻鬟松④。
醒时空对烛花红。

Washing Brook Sand

Filling in the deep cup by strong wine in pink,
Let me greedy to drink till I am deeply drunk.
The wind seems a late partner to have the bell work.

The borneol fragrance lost, my lovesick dream broken,
The small gold ornament in my hair-bun, easily loosen.
Waking up, lonely I look at the candle to burn.

【译注】

①莫许：不要。琥珀浓：酒的颜色呈褐色或红褐色。
②疏钟：断续的钟声。
③瑞脑：一种熏香的名字，也叫龙脑，即冰片。
④辟寒金：相传三国魏明帝时，昆明国进贡嗽金鸟，此鸟居避寒台，吐金屑如粟。宫人争以鸟吐之金饰钗佩，谓之“辟寒金”。这里泛指精金头饰。髻鬟：古代妇女的两种发式。

浣溪沙

小院闲窗①春色深，
重帘未卷影沉沉②。
倚楼无语理瑶琴③。

远岫④出山催薄暮，
细风吹雨弄轻阴⑤。
梨花欲谢恐难禁。

Washing Brook Sand

The deep spring at a small courtyard with a free window,
The thick curtain not fallen, the maiden left her dark shadow.
Voicelessly, she was playing her ancient zither solo.

In the thin twilight, standing was the distant mountain,
The mildly-blowing wind scattered the lingering rain.
It is hard to stop pear blossoms continuously fallen.

【译注】

①闲窗：带护栏的窗子。闲：遮拦阻隔之物，阑也。
②沉沉：幽暗，影子浓重。
③瑶琴：一般指有玉饰的琴。
④岫（xiù）：山有穴称"岫"。这里泛指山峰。远岫：远山。
⑤轻阴：暗淡的轻云。

浣溪沙

淡荡春光寒食天，
玉炉沉水①袅残烟。
梦回山枕隐花钿②。

海燕未来人斗草③，
江梅已过柳生绵。
黄昏疏雨湿秋千。

Washing Brook Sand

Spring sunshine is with vividly light on Cold Food Day,
Out of the censer residual incenses' smokes curl lazily.
My dream hid in U-shaped pillow with the hair inlay.

Kids played grass-picking-up game, no sea swallows fly,
River-plums withered, catkins continuously float in the sky.
The lingering drizzle wetted the swing at the twilight.

【译注】

①玉炉：香炉之美称。沉水：香料名，又称沉水香，简称沉香。

②山枕：两端隆起中间低凹如山形的凹枕。花钿（diàn）：用金片镶嵌成花形的首饰。

③斗草：一种竞采百草以赛优胜的游戏。

浣溪沙

闺情①

绣面芙蓉②一笑开，
斜飞宝鸭③衬香腮。
眼波才动被人猜。

一面风情深有韵，
半笺娇恨寄幽怀。
月移花影约重来。

Washing Brook Sand

Maiden Affection

Her pretty face is like a broidered lotus with a smile,
A duck-pendant suspended to her cheek as a foil.
Double eyes rolled as if her reciting a lyric.

One side of her body looked romantic,
Half a lyric piece of paper sent to talk mind.
The flowery shadow under moon hinted invite.

【译注】

①《浣溪沙》：词牌名。唐玄宗时教坊曲名，后用为词牌，亦作《浣溪纱》。分平仄两体，字数以四十二字居多，还有四十四字和四十六字两种。全词分两片，上片三句全用韵，下片末二句用韵。曲调轻松明快，是宋词中使用频率较高的词牌名。

②绣面：面容姣美。芙蓉：荷花，此处指面容好看像荷花盛开了。

③斜飞宝鸭：指女人发髻装饰物。当时的妇女多有向脸上贴绣习惯。

凤凰台上忆吹箫①

香冷金猊②，被翻红浪③，
起来慵自梳头。
任宝奁④尘满，日上帘钩。
生怕离怀别苦，多少事、欲说还休。
新来瘦，非干病酒，不是悲秋。

休休！这回去也，千万遍阳关⑤，
也则难留。
念武陵人远⑥，烟锁秦楼⑦。
惟有楼前流水，应念我、终日凝眸。
凝眸处，从今又添，一段新愁。

【译注】

①《凤凰台上忆吹箫》词牌名又称为《忆吹箫》。其寓意来自春秋时秦穆公的女儿弄玉和其夫萧史的故事。弄玉善吹箫，秦穆公为她建凤台，使夫妻居于台上。几年之后，弄玉乘凤，萧史乘龙飞走。

②金猊（ní）：狮形铜香炉。

③红浪：红色被铺乱摊在床上，有如波浪。

④宝奁（lián）：华贵的梳妆镜匣。

Recalling Flute Song on Phoenix Terrace

Gold censer with burning incenses were getting colder,
My quilt like red waves thrown upside in disorder,
Getting up, still I felt too sleepy and lazy to comb hair.
No matter how much dust covered on makeup desk,
The morning sun still climbed upon the curtain hook.
Afraid of parting, my mind full of lovesick pain,
How many romantic memories happened again?
Willingly to recall, but stop in vain.
Recently I have been thin,
I am greedy to drink a cup of wine,
But not for the gloomy autumn again.

No, no, this time, no need to drink alcohol!
Thousands of farewell songs could not stop to go.
Imagining one Wuling man ① to leave off afar,
Yet the mist still locked my watchtower.
Only in front of my building, a brook in flow,
Knew where I knit my brows.
From now on to add a new sorrow.

⑤阳关：语出《阳关三叠》，是唐宋时著名的送别曲。

⑥武陵人远：此处一说引用陶渊明《桃花源记》武陵郡渔人误入桃花源，离开后再去便找不到路径了的典故。一说用刘晨、阮肇桃林仙境遇仙女并与之相会的典故。

⑦秦楼：指秦穆公之女弄玉与恋人萧史所居之楼（详见《列仙传》）。此处借指李清照与赵明诚所居之楼。

【Annotation】

① one Wuling man: quoted from great writer and poet Tao Yuanming's *Peach Blossom Spring*, Wuling fisherman came into the Peach Blossom Spring, left and then could not find the cave exit.

一剪梅

红藕香残玉簟秋，
轻解罗裳，独上兰舟。
云中谁寄锦书来?
雁字回时，月满西楼。

花自飘零水自流，
一种相思，两处闲愁。
此情无计可消除，
才下眉头，却上心头。

A Blooming Plum

The fragrant red lotuses have withered away,
My jade-like mat turns cool on autumn day,
Lightly putting off my skirt or silky coat,
Alone I boarded on the pretty boat.
Looking back, the wild geese fly,
Who's to send me a letter through clouds' sky?
My west chamber window's full of moonlight.

Flowers drift alone out of the smell,
The creek running alone is natural,
There's one kind of lovesickness,
Coming from two places with sadness.
No way could cure such a sickness,
Just falling down from my eyebrows,
Into my heart with sorrows.

蝶恋花
晚止昌乐馆寄姊妹

泪湿罗衣脂粉满[1]，
四叠阳关[2]，
唱到[3]千千遍。
人道山长山又断，
萧萧微雨闻孤馆。

惜别伤离方寸[4]乱，
忘了临行，
酒盏深和浅。
好把音书凭过雁，
东莱不似蓬莱远。

Butterflies Fallen in Love with Flowers

Tears were falling down on my cheek and silk gown,
Time and time again I sang a farewell lyric song,
To be lasting for thousand times long.
It was told the long mountain would be broken,
The lonely guesthouse heard of lingering rain.

It was a pity my heart was full of sorrow,
I did not know my cup being deep or shallow.
I would ask the flying wild geese to mail a few lines,
For Donglai was not so far away as Penglai paradise.

【译注】

①湿：《花草粹编》作"挹"。罗：《翰墨大全》作"征"。满：《花草粹编》作"暖"。罗：一种丝织品。

②阳关：指王维《送元二使安西》诗，此诗和乐后成为送别名曲。之所以称为"三叠"，是因为按照曲谱的规定，"西出阳关无故人"一句在演唱时应反复三遍，以表现依依惜别之情，此处称四叠意为唱了无数遍的送别曲。

③唱：《历代诗余》作"听"。到：《花草粹编》作"了"。

④方寸：指心。

蝶恋花

暖雨晴风初破冻[1]，
柳眼梅腮[2]，
已觉春心[3]动。
酒意诗情谁与共？
泪融残粉花钿重。

乍试夹衫金缕缝[4]，
山枕斜欹[5]，
枕损钗头凤。
独抱浓愁无好梦，
夜阑犹剪灯花弄[6]。

【译注】

①雨：《乐府雅词》作“日”，旁注“雨”。晴：一作“和”或“清”。

②眼：一作“润”。腮：一作“轻”。

③春心：被春景触动的心思。

④夹衫金缕缝：用金线缝制的夹衫。

⑤欹（qī）：通“倚”，斜依，斜靠。

⑥夜阑：夜深。灯花：灯芯余烬结成的花形。

Butterflies Fallen in Love with Flowers

The winter ice began to melt with the warm
breeze and rain,
Willows' eyes opened, plum blossoms turned
red again,
Spring heart already felt fast-beaten.
Who would share my intoxicated sense or
lyrics?
Tears rolled down on my cheeks' powders.

My gold-flowery hairpin seemed heavy,
I tried to wear my shirt sewn by gold threads,
Then lying on my U- shaped pillow slantingly,
My phoenix-hairpin broken up abruptly.
Alone embracing thick melancholy meant no
good dream,
The night going over, I still made the candle
flower bloom.

鹧鸪天

暗淡轻黄体性柔，
情疏迹远只香留。
何须①浅碧深红色，
自是②花中第一流。

梅定妒，菊应羞，
画阑开处冠中秋。
骚人可煞③无情思，
何事当年不见收。

The Partridge Sky

The flowery osmanthus look dim, light and yellow,
Her emotion is thin, lonely with fully fragrant flow.
It is unnecessary to be so deep red, so light green,
She is sure of such a kind of blossom queen.

Plum blossoms envy, chrysanthemum shameful,
In mid-autumn, osmanthus is the most beautiful.
As a poet, you could be very inconsiderate,
Why you had no such osmanthus to collect.

【译注】

①何须：何必。

②自是：本来是。

③可煞（kě shà）：亦作“可杀”，表示疑问，犹可是，是否；也表示极甚之辞，犹言非常。

小重山[1]

春到长门[2]春草青，
红梅些子[3]破，
未开匀。
碧云笼碾玉成尘[4]，
留晓梦，
惊破一瓯春。

花影压重门，
疏帘铺淡月，
好黄昏。
二年三度负东君[5]，
归来也，
著意过今春。

【译注】

①小重山：词牌名，古人常用以写“宫怨”，亦作“小重山令”。

②长门：西汉宫殿名。汉武帝的陈皇后因妒失宠，被遣居长门宫。后以长门代失宠后妃所居冷宫。

③些子：一些，少许。

④碧云笼碾玉成尘：徐培均《李清照集笺注》谓：“宋人饮茶，碾碎再罗，然后入汤。”碧云：青绿色的团茶。笼：碾茶的器具。玉成尘：指翠绿的茶叶被碾成碎末的形状。

⑤东君：原为《楚辞·九歌》篇名，以东君为日神，后演变为春神。词中指美好的春光。

The Overlapping Hill

Spring came in the palace gate, the grass green,
A little bit red plum blossoms were open,
Yet the color was not red enough to get even.
The emerald-like tea-cake was crashed thin,
The morning dream remained to make spring shock.

Flowers' shadow pressed on the door with a plunk,
The curtain kept away from the pale moon,
That's a wonderful dusk.
I'm sorry to be unworthy of you, East Spring Girl,
I wish you to go home,
This year, let us share the vernal.

怨王孙[①]

湖上风来波浩渺，
秋已暮、红[②]稀香少。
水光山色与人亲，
说不尽、无穷好。

莲子已成荷叶老，
清露洗、蘋花汀草[③]。
眠沙鸥鹭不回头，
似也恨、人归早。

Lyrics for King Posterity

Over the vast lake, the gale was to blow,
Wave upon wave, billow upon billow,
It's the late autumn now,
Fewer flowers red with less fragrant smell.
The river is brighter, the mountain prettier,
The human people dear,
It's endless to be praised, endlessly better.

Lotus seeds ripe, the leafs old in yellow,
Lake shore's flowers or grass washed by the dew.
The sleepy gulls were not looking back on beach,
As if hating the coming man not early to go.

【译注】
①怨王孙：词牌名，又名《忆君王》《忆王孙》。
②红：指代花。
③蘋：多年生水草。汀：水边平地。

临江仙（一）

庭院深深深几许？
云窗雾阁常扃[①]。
柳梢梅萼渐分明。
春归秣陵[②]树，
人老建康城。

感月吟风多少事，
如今老去无成。
谁怜憔悴更凋零。
试灯无意思，
踏雪没心情。

【译注】

李清照这首词有两个版本，不好判定哪首为正统，这里一并译出，供读者参考。

①扃（jiōng）：上闩，关闭。

②秣陵：指今江苏南京。

Riverside Fairy Maiden

One

How deep is the deep courtyard extension?
The cloud and fog often lock windows or the pavilion.
The willow top and plum calyxes were clearly seen.
Spring would be back to an ancient city's tree,
The aged man would like to make the city healthy.

How many romances happened to the wind-moon,
Nowadays I am too old to do something pretty soon.
Who shows a sympathy to my haggard spirits in low?
Testing the lantern is meaningless now,
Also no enthusiasm to tread the snow.

临江仙（二）

梅

庭院深深深几许，
云窗雾阁春迟。
为谁憔悴损芳姿？
夜来清梦好，
应是发南枝。

玉瘦檀轻①无限恨，
南楼羌管②休吹。
浓香吹尽有谁知，
暖风迟日③也，
别到杏花肥④。

【译注】

①玉瘦檀轻：谓梅花姿态清瘦，颜色浅红。
②羌管：羌笛。
③暖风迟日：春风温暖、阳光柔和。
④肥：《历代诗余》等作“时”。

Riverside Fairy Maiden

Two

How deep is the deep courtyard extension?
Late spring's clouds shroud windows or the pavilion.
For whom? You look so haggard and so slim!
Dreaming a clear good dream,
Should originate from south twigs of plum.

Slightly fragrant bed knew my body thin,
With my endless hatred to deepen,
The Qiang-flute singing stopped in south-pavilion.
The wind will puff off thick fragrance, no one knows,
The day will gradually last longer with the warm breeze,
Till the apricot is full of blossoms.

醉花阴

薄雾浓云愁永昼①，
瑞脑销金兽②。
佳节又重阳，
玉枕纱厨③，
半夜凉初透。

东篱④把酒黄昏后，
有暗香⑤盈袖。
莫道不销魂⑥，
帘卷西风⑦，
人比黄花⑧瘦。

Being Intoxicated in Flowery Shade

The mist thin, the cloud thick,
I have been melancholy since the daybreak,
In censer, the fragrant incenses burnt.
It's the Double-Ninth Festival again,
My jade pillow shrouded by the silk curtain,
The midnight coldness is to deepen.

Looking at homely fence to drink after dusk,
The autumn fragrance is hidden in sleeves' dark.
Do not say that is not gloomy to my soul,
The curtain rolling up, autumn winds blow,
My body is leaner than the flower in yellow.

【译注】

①永昼：漫长的白天。
②金兽：兽形的铜香炉。
③纱厨：纱帐。
④东篱：泛指赏菊之地，取自陶渊明《饮酒》诗："采菊东篱下，悠然见南山。"
⑤暗香：这里指菊花的幽香。古诗《庭中有奇树》："攀条折其荣，将以遗所思。馨香盈怀袖，路远莫致之。"这里用其意。
⑥销魂：指因思念而产生的黯然情绪。
⑦帘卷西风：西风卷帘。
⑧黄花：菊花。

好事近

风定落花深，
帘外拥红堆雪①。
长记海棠开后，
正是伤春时节。

酒阑②歌罢玉尊空，
青缸暗明灭③。
魂梦不堪幽怨，
更一声啼鴂④。

【译注】

①拥红堆雪：凋落的有红有白的花瓣聚集堆积。

②酒阑：喝完了酒。五代毛文锡《恋情深》："酒阑歌罢两沉沉，一笑动君心。"宋李冠《蝶恋花》："愁破酒阑闺梦熟，月斜窗外风敲竹。"

③青缸：青灯，即灯火青荧，灯光青白微弱之意。《广韵》："缸，灯。"缸：《花草粹编》等作"红"。暗明灭：指灯光忽明忽暗，一直到熄灭。

④鴂（jué）：即鹈鴂。宋辛弃疾《贺新郎》词："绿树听鹈鴂，更那堪、鹧鸪声住，杜鹃声切。"

Something Lovely to Happen Soon

The wind in no blow, deeply-falling flowers follow,
Outside curtains, red flowers covered by the snow.
Long memories of begonia being open,
Still melancholy, I recall the spring season.

As singing is over, the jade cup turns empty,
The lamp seems either bright but gloomy.
My soul dream could not bear my melancholy sigh,
Still I had to listen to a partridge's cry.

诉衷情

夜来沉醉卸妆迟，
梅萼[1]插残枝。
酒醒熏破春睡，
梦远不成归。

人悄悄[2]，
月依依，
翠帘垂。
更挼[3]残蕊，
更捻[4]余香，
更得些时。

Telling Inner Feelings

Night, the tipsy maiden had her makeup clean,
A plum blossom was inserted in her hair-bun.
Being sober, she had her spring sleep break,
But her dream was too far to come back.

The girl kept quiet,
The moon scanned her light,
The jade-pearl curtain rolled down at night.
With her fingers, she twisted residual plum pistil,
As if twisting the residual fragrant smell,
And doing so for a little bit time still.

【译注】

①梅萼：梅的萼片，此处代指梅。

②悄悄：忧愁的样子。化用《诗经·邶风·柏舟》的“忧心悄悄”等句意，也可能是借鉴了五代顾敻（xiòng）《献衷心》一词（顾词有“人悄悄，月明时。想昔年欢笑，恨今日分离”等句）。

③挼（ruó）：揉搓。

④捻：用手搓转，其揉搓程度比“挼”更进一层。

行香子[①]
七夕

草际鸣蛩[②]，惊落梧桐，
正人间、天上愁浓。
云阶月地[③]，关锁千重。
纵浮槎[④]来，浮槎去，不相逢。

星桥鹊驾[⑤]，经年才见，
想离情、别恨难穷。
牵牛织女[⑥]，莫是离中。
甚霎儿晴[⑦]，霎儿雨，霎儿风。

【译注】

①行香子：词牌名。双调小令，六十六字，上片五平韵，下片四平韵。

②蛩（qióng）：（古）蟋蟀。

③云阶月地：指天宫。语出杜牧《七夕》："云阶月地一相过，未抵经年别恨多。"

④槎（chá）：用竹木编成的筏子。浮槎：传说中指往来于海上和天河之间的木筏。（张华《博物志》记载，天河与海可通，每年八月有浮槎，来往从不失期。有人矢志要上天宫，带了许多吃食浮槎而往，航行十数天竟到达了天河。此人看到牛郎在河边饮牛，织女却在很遥远的天宫中。）

⑤星桥鹊驾：传说七夕牛郎织女在天河相会时，喜鹊为之搭桥，故称鹊桥。

⑥牵牛织女：天上二星宿名。曹植《九咏》注曰："牵牛为夫，织女为妇。"

⑦甚：怎，何。霎儿：一会儿。

Going to Burn Incenses for Buddha

In grass, crickets chirp to make Indus lofty
leaves fall low,
It's time that the human world or the paradise
in sorrow.
From cloudy steps to the moon's surface,
There are thousands of passes with locks.
Although rafts were floating back and forth,
Still there was no reunion-meeting way or
path.

Magpies would set up a starry bridge in a
year,
How long for both of them to meet together?
The Cowboy and the Weaving Girl were
bitterly separated from each other.
Sometimes it's a very fine day,
And then it may be rainy or windy.

行香[1]子

天与秋光，转转情伤，
探金英知近重阳。
薄衣初试，绿蚁[2]新尝，
渐一番风，一番雨，一番凉。

黄昏院落，凄凄惶惶，
酒醒时往事愁肠。
那堪永夜，明月空床。
闻砧[3]声捣，蛩声细，漏声长。

Going to Burn Incenses for Buddha

It's the sky with the autumn sight,
And a love-sick sigh.
Looking up at the chrysanthemum in yellow,
I know it's the coming Double-Ninth Festival.
The first try is to put on my thin gown,
A cup of wonderful wine is to drink on,
Gradually to happen is a gust of gale,
A burst of drizzle,
A sky of cool.

The yard twilight looks yellow,
I'm desolate in silent sorrow,
Then sober, my mind full of past trouble.
There's no everlasting night,
Over my empty bed, hovers the moon light.
Being heard of anvil-sounding pound,
Crickets chirp a little bit louder,
An ancient timer clicks much longer.

【译注】

①行香：正月初一清早，旧有“行香”之俗，始于晋代道安法师。所谓“行香”之俗就是竞先赶到社庙或寺院里开殿门和烧头香，点香灯。

②绿蚁：一种新酿成的酒，上浮绿色泡沫。

③砧：古代捣衣用的石头。

孤雁儿[①]

（世人作梅词，下笔便俗。予试作一篇，乃知前言不妄耳。）

藤床纸帐[②]朝眠起，
说不尽、无佳思[③]。
沉香烟断玉炉寒[④]，
伴我情怀如水。
笛声三弄[⑤]，
梅心惊破[⑥]，
多少春情意[⑦]。

小风疏雨潇潇地[⑧]，
又催下、千行泪。
吹箫人去[⑨]玉楼空，
肠断[⑩]与谁同倚？
一枝折得，
人间天上，
没个人堪寄[⑪]。

A Lonely Wild Goose

(Whoever was to write a plum blooming lyric, such a writing would be vulgar; if necessary to have a try, anyone should accept such a lesson.)

Awaken from rattan-bed shrouded by silken curtain,
There're endless words to tell of no good emotion.
Incenses stopped burning, jade censer got colder,
Smoke accompanying my mind like cool water.
Playing the flute repeatedly,
Let plum blossoms shocked suddenly,
How affectionate is spring day!

The breeze was lightly in blow,
The sparse drizzles seemed to rustle,
To urge my tears fully to flow.
The flute player left afar,
My chamber remained emptier.
Whom I would lean upon,
When my heart was broken.
Breaking off a twig of weeping willow,
Dedicated to whom, no one knew,
Either in paradise or in globe.

【译注】

①孤雁儿：此词有序言，也被后人称为《孤雁儿·并序》，是李清照晚年时期的作品，写于丈夫赵明诚去世之后。《孤雁儿》原名《御街行》，《古今词话》载有变格一首，中有"听

孤雁，声嘹唳”句，故更名《孤雁儿》。
②藤床：藤条编织的床。纸帐：用藤皮茧纸做的帐子。
③佳思：好心情。
④沉香：薰香的一种。玉炉：玉制的香炉或是香炉的代称。
⑤三弄：即“梅花三弄”，古代笛曲名，或称“梅花引”。
⑥梅心：梅花的苞蕾。惊破：梅花花苞初绽。
⑦春情意：喻指当年夫妻情深。
⑧潇潇地：淅淅沥沥。地，语助词。
⑨吹箫人去：据《列仙传》：“萧史者，秦穆公时人也，善吹箫，能致孔雀、白鹤于庭。穆公有女字弄玉，好之。公遂以女妻焉。”此句暗指其夫赵明诚已经去世。
⑩肠断：这里形容因丧夫而悲伤之极。《世说新语·黜免》：“桓公入蜀，至三峡中，部伍中有得猿子者，其母缘岸哀号，行百余里，不去，遂跳上船，至便即绝。破视其腹中，肠皆寸寸断。”
⑪“一枝折得”三句：化用陆凯《赠范晔诗》诗意。折梅相送，丈夫故去，所以说没人堪寄。

满庭芳

小阁藏春，闲窗锁昼，
画堂无限深幽。
篆香[①]烧尽，日影下帘钩[②]。
手种江梅[③]更好，又何必、临水登楼[④]？
无人到，寂寥恰似[⑤]、何逊在扬州[⑥]。

从来，知韵胜[⑦]，难堪雨藉[⑧]，不耐风揉[⑨]。
更谁家横笛[⑩]，吹动浓愁？
莫恨香消玉减，须信道、扫迹情留[⑪]。
难言处，良宵淡月，疏影[⑫]尚风流。

【译注】

①篆香：对盘香的喻称，一说指“一种印有篆文的熏香”。
②帘钩：挂帘的钩子。
③江梅：指梅中上品，非泛指江畔、水边之梅。
④临水登楼：指思念家乡。
⑤寂寥：寂静、空旷。恰似：简直像，完全像。
⑥何逊在扬州：何逊，南朝梁诗人。语出杜

The Courtyard[①] Full of Fragrance

Spring was silently hidden in the Small Pavilion,
The sunshine locked outside by the window screen,
The quiet painting hall seemed infinitively to deepen.
The Buddhist incenses burnt out till no smoke,
The sun's shadow was under the curtain hook.
It is the plum blossoms I planted better than the other,
Why still were you upstairs to waterside to have a look?
No one came in my home,
My mind's full of sorrow,
Now I'm pitiful to stay at Yangzhou.

With plum blossoms always wonderful,
I am troubled by the drizzle,
And unbearable of the gale.
Whose long horizontal flute in play to make me seriously melancholy?
No hatred of lost fragrance to follow,
Though few plum blossoms like snow,
Be sure of your way!
There's no plum blooming trace to remain.

甫《和裴迪登蜀州东亭送客逢早梅相忆见寄》诗：“东阁官梅动诗兴，还如何逊在扬州。”《全芳备祖》卷一《花部梅花纪要》载：“梁何逊在扬州法曹，廨舍有梅花一枝，逊吟咏其下。后居洛思梅花，再请其任，从之。抵扬州，花方盛，逊对花彷徨。”

⑦韵胜：指梅花的风韵逸群，超出一般。

⑧难堪雨藉：难以承受雨打。藉：踏，这里指侵害。

⑨不耐风揉：《乐府雅词》卷下、《梅苑》卷三、《全宋词》第二册均作“不耐风柔”，“柔”字不通，故改。

⑩笛：指汉横吹曲中《梅花落》。

⑪扫迹情留：语见孔稚珪《北山移文》：“乍低枝而扫迹。”原意为扫除干净，不留痕迹。此处系反其意而用之。

⑫ 疏影：梅花稀疏的影子。

What's hardly to say?
The night moonlight left her shadow,
Still romantic and beautiful.

[Annotation]

① courtyard here used as a noun to refer the front yard.

玉楼春[①]
红梅

红酥肯放琼苞碎[②]，
探著南枝开遍未。
不知酝藉[③]几多香，
但见包藏无限意。

道人憔悴[④]春窗底，
闷损阑干愁不倚。
要来小酌便来休[⑤]，
未必明朝风不起。

Spring in Marble Pavilion

Red plum blossoms bloom, tiny buds open,
I wonder if all the sunny-side twigs bloom again.
I do not know how much fragrance in air,
Yet the unlimited love hints can be seen.

The haggard Taoist stayed at the spring window bottom,
Not leaning upon the balustrade with depressed boredom.
To come to drink a little bit for a fun,
Tomorrow the wind may blow up again.

【译注】

①玉楼春：词牌名，又名《木兰花》。

②红酥：这里指色泽红润的梅花。琼苞：像玉一般温润欲放的鲜嫩梅蕊。

③酝藉：《汉书·薛广德传》：“广德为人，温雅有酝藉。”意谓宽和、涵容。在此词中则与下句的“包藏”意思相近。

④道人：一说“道人”为李清照自指；一说“道”指“议论”，“人”是李清照自指，合起来意为别人议论我；一说“道人”指知人。憔悴：困顿萎靡的样子。

⑤小酌：随便的饮宴。休：语助词，含有“呵”的意思。便来休：张相《诗词曲语辞汇释》卷三：“此犹云快来呵。”

渔家傲
记梦

天接云涛连晓雾，
星河欲转千帆舞①。
仿佛梦魂归帝所②。
闻天语，
殷勤问我归何处。

我报路长嗟日暮③，
学诗谩有④惊人句。
九万里风鹏正举⑤。
风休住，
蓬舟吹取三山去⑥。

【译注】

①星河：银河。转：移换位置。
②帝所：天帝住的宫殿。
③报：回答。嗟（jiē）：悲叹，叹息。
④谩（màn）有：空有。
⑤九万里风鹏正举：语本《庄子·逍遥游》：“鹏之徙于南冥也，水击三千里，抟扶摇而上者九万里。”举：高飞。
⑥蓬舟：轻如蓬草的小船。吹取：吹得，吹到。三山：古代神话，东方大海里有三座仙山，叫作蓬莱、方丈、瀛洲。

Fisherman Proud

The cloud waves fly to the foggy sky in the morning,
The stars saw the Milky Way help boats sail like dancing.
I dreamed of going back to paradise to rest my soul.
Listening to my God blessing echo,
And answering God where I would like to go.

Looking over the long road, I made a sigh to the coming twilight,
Learning much longer, I had no wonderful poem to write.
One myth-bird could fly 90,000-miles in heaven.
The blowing gale should never stop again,
To sail the myth-boat to the Penglai Island of the Three-Mountain.

清平乐[①]

年年雪里，
常插梅花醉。
挼尽梅花无好意[②]，
赢得[③]满衣清泪。

今年海角天涯，
萧萧两鬓生华。
看取[④]晚来风势，
故应难看梅花。

Purely Monotonous Music

Year by year, in snowing, plum blossoms bloom,
Happily inserting the blossom in bun hair I comb.
The plum blossoms' soul seemed to be gone,
My gown immersed by crystal tears rolling down.

This year we are apart each other far far away,
My both temples have silently turned gray.
The late evening wind tendency seemed to be strong,
It may be difficult to see the plum bloom much long.

【译注】

①这首词是李清照后期的名篇。往昔赏梅，今日怜梅，展示了作者不同时期的不同境遇，表现了身世飘零的不幸，寄托着深沉的家国之忧，思想内容远较一般的咏梅词深广。

②挼（ruó）：揉搓。无好意：没遇上好机会，心情不好。

③赢得：剩得。

④看取：观察。

鹧鸪天

寒日萧萧上琐窗[1]，
梧桐应恨夜来霜。
酒阑更喜团茶苦[2]，
梦断偏宜瑞脑香[3]。

秋已尽，日犹长，
仲宣[4]怀远更凄凉。
不如随分尊前醉[5]，
莫负东篱菊蕊黄[6]。

The Partridge Sky

The wooden window was with rustling cold daylight,
The parasol-like leaves seemed to hate frosty night.
The wine drunk dry, I'd like a cup of bitter tea,
My residual broken dream remained sweet tasty.

Autumn was over, the day would last long,
Writer Wang Tsan's optimistic memories were gone.
I prefer to intoxicate to hold a cup of wine,
Than to let yellow daisy pistils in sad sigh.

【译注】

①萧萧：凄清冷落的样子。原为拟声词，如风声、雨声、草木摇落声、马蹄声。《诗经·小雅·车攻》有"萧萧马鸣"，《楚辞·九怀·蓄英》有"秋风兮萧萧"，《史记·刺客列传》有"风萧萧兮易水寒"。琐窗：镂刻连锁纹饰的窗户。
②酒阑：酒尽，酒酣。阑：残，尽，晚。司马迁《史记·高祖本纪》有"酒阑"，裴骃集解曰："阑，言希（同稀）也，谓饮酒者半罢半在，谓之阑。"《文选·谢庄〈宋孝武宣贵妃诔〉》有"白露凝兮岁将阑"，李善注曰"阑，犹晚也"。团茶：团片状的压缩

茶饼，饮用时碾碎。宋代有龙团、凤团、小龙团等多种品种，比较名贵。欧阳修《归田录》卷二："茶之品，莫贵于龙凤，谓之团茶，凡八饼重一斤。"

③瑞脑：即龙涎香，又名龙脑香。

④仲宣：王粲，字仲宣，汉末文学家，"建安七子"之一。作《登楼赋》抒发怀念故土及才高不遇之情。

⑤随分：随便，随意。尊前：指宴席上。尊，同"樽"。

⑥东篱菊蕊黄：化用陶渊明《饮酒二十首》的"采菊东篱下"句。

添字丑奴儿

窗前谁种芭蕉树?
阴满中庭。
阴满中庭,
叶叶心心,
舒卷有余情。

伤心枕上三更雨,
点滴霖霪。
点滴霖霪,
愁损北人,
不惯起来听!

Homology Variant of Comic Clown

Who planted the banana tree in front of the window?
The courtyard was overcast by the shadow.
The courtyard was overcast by the shadow,
Leaf to leaf is like heart to heart,
Their lovely vivid manners show not to be apart.

The sad pillow heard of the midnight rain,
Drop by drop, falling down time and again.
Drip by drip, falling down time and again,
It's an excessive rain to let the Northland gloomy,
That broke the people's habits to be sleepy.

忆秦娥

临高阁，
乱山平野烟光薄。
烟光薄，
栖鸦归后，
暮天闻角。

断香残酒情怀恶，
西风催衬梧桐落。
梧桐落，
又还秋色，
又还寂寞。

Recalling Maiden Qin'E

Upstairs to the lofty Pavilion,
I look over the disorderly mountain, plain,
Being shrouded by light smoke,
By light smoke,
The returned crows settled down,
In the twilight I heard of the horn.

The incenses burnt to an end, the wine left a little,
Being in low spirits, I felt evil,
The parasol tree leaves were fallen by the west wind-blow.
The parasol tree leaves were fallen by the west wind-blow,
The autumn scenery was given back again,
My loneliness was given me back again.

念奴娇
春情

萧条庭院，
又斜风细雨，
重门须闭。
宠柳娇花寒食近，
种种恼人天气。
险韵[①]诗成，
扶头酒[②]醒，
别是闲滋味。
征鸿过尽，
万千心事难寄。

楼上几日春寒，
帘垂四面，
玉阑干[③]慵倚。
被冷香消[④]新梦觉，
不许愁人不起。
清露晨流，
新桐初引[⑤]，
多少游春意。
日高烟敛，
更看今日晴未？

A Pretty Dancing Girl

The courtyard looked desolate, bleak,
The breeze seemed slant, the drizzle, tick by tick,
Going on, not to stop.
The inner door was shut up.
Willows mild, flowers lovely,
It's the coming Cold Food Holiday,
All kinds of annoying weather let me melancholy.
An exceptional rhyme formed in mind,
I was sober from the strong wine,
To leave me pleasure inside.
Far-flying geese vanished into the sky,
They could hardly to mail my myriad love senses in mind.

In recent days, upstairs I feel chill cold,
The window curtains roll down low,
I am lazy to lean upon jade railing pillow.
The quilt cool, incenses burnt to an end,
I woke up from a new dream land,
Helplessly suffering into sorrow,
unwilling to leave off my pillow.
Just looking at the morning dew,
The new parasol-like leaves begin to grow.
How I wish to have a spring travel!

【译注】

①险韵：以生僻字协韵写诗填词。

The sun is rising up high,
The cooking smoke is getting low,
Today is sunny or not, I'd like to know.

②扶头酒：能让人精神振作的好酒，饮多则易醉。一说“扶头”为酒名。
③玉阑干：白石栏杆。
④香消：香炉中的香已烧尽。
⑤初引：初长。

永遇乐

落日熔金①，
暮云合璧②，
人在何处？
染柳烟浓，
吹梅笛怨，
春意知几许？
元宵佳节，
融和天气，
次第岂无风雨？
来相召，
香车宝马，
谢他酒朋诗侣。

中州③盛日，
闺门多暇，
记得偏重三五④。
铺翠冠儿⑤，
捻金雪柳，
簇带争济楚。
如今憔悴，
风鬟雾鬓，
怕见夜间出去。
不如向、
帘儿底下，
听人笑语。

Pleasure for Perpetual Reunion

The setting sun was molten into the golden light,
Well-combined were the dyed clouds and twilight,
Where might be seen the maiden sight?
The weeping willows seemed to be in green dye,
To be shrouded by the mist under the blue sky,
The flute played "Plum Blossoms Fallen" song,
That's full of spring smell much strong.
It's on the joyous Lantern Festival,
The wind is mild and gentle,
In natural sequence turn, there must be a drizzle, and a personnel reunion as well.
Writers or poets would board on a horse-driven luxurious wagon,
Be grateful to pen pals time and again.

On the Song Dynasty's heyday in Bianliang Capital,
In the boudoir, maidens were much free, joyful,
I remember all of them were cheerful when the moon full.
The maiden's hat inlaid with the orb of emerald,
Her body ornament was with a golden-snowy-

willow,
What she wore seemed extremely beautiful.
Nowadays the maiden haggard,
Both her hair bun or temples in disorder,
At night she was afraid to go outside.
She felt better to stay under the curtain,
Listening to laugh at her by any person.

【译注】

①落日熔金：日落时金黄灿烂的颜色。

②暮云合璧：日落后，红霞消散，暮云像碧玉般合成一片。

③中州：指北宋都城汴京，今河南开封。

④三五：古人常称阴历十五为“三五”，此处代指元宵节。

⑤铺翠冠儿：上面装饰着碧翠羽毛的帽子。

长寿乐

南昌生日[1]

（存疑之作）

微寒应候，望日边，六叶阶蓂初秀[2]。
爱景欲挂扶桑[3]，漏残银箭[4]，杓回摇斗[5]。
庆高闳[6]此际，掌上一颗明珠剖。
有令容淑质，归逢佳偶。
到如今，昼锦[7]满堂贵胄。

荣耀，文步紫禁[8]，一一金章绿绶[9]。
更值棠棣连阴[10]，虎符熊轼[11]，夹河分守[12]。
况青云咫尺[13]，朝暮重入承明[14]后。
看彩衣争献[15]，兰羞玉酎[16]。
祝千龄，借指松椿比寿[17]。

Longevity Music

It is a slightly cold day as the winter goes on,
At the heavenly end, the full moon hung,
In courtyard front, the six-leaf grass grew up young.
The lovely scenery lay over a fairy tree,
The water-pot timer pointed to a lower degree,
The Big Dipper's handle showed it's a spring day.
On the triumphal arc for celebration,
There must be a bright pearl of decoration.
Nancy used to be beautiful and gentle,
With a good guy to be a good couple.
Nowadays he put on a gown to go to hometown,
To see the noble family members, old or young.

It was glorious for him to step to the palace,
Holding his gold seal with green ribbons.
Nancy's two sons appointed as high officials,
Ordered to defend the native land and rivers.
As if lofty clouds close at hand, they have good luck,
Moreover, both were promoted to be in higher rank.
She put on colorful costume to brighten the party,
With delicious foods and drinks for the aged

【译注】

①南昌生日：这是首寿词，南昌乃是寿主韩肖胄母亲的诰命。（诰命：皇帝封赠官员的专用文书。）

②应候：顺应时令。六叶阶蓂（míng）：蓂荚是古代传说的祥瑞之草。每月初一到十五，每日结一荚；从十六到月终，每日落一荚。由

此可知道是何日。此处指寿主的生日是初六。
③爱景：指冬日的太阳。扶桑：神话中的树木名。
④漏：即漏壶，是古代一种计时器，壶内壁有刻度。银箭：指银饰的标记时刻以计时的漏箭。
⑤杓（biāo）回摇斗：斗柄向东折回，指春天即将来到。
⑥高闳（hóng）：高大的门。这里指显贵门第。
⑦昼锦：通常指古代显贵或官宦衣锦还乡。《汉书·项籍传》："富贵不归故乡，如衣锦夜行。"这里或指韩肖胄曾祖韩琦所建昼锦堂。
⑧紫禁：以紫微星垣比喻皇帝的居处，故称皇宫为紫禁。
⑨金章绿绶：金章，以金为印章。绿绶，印柄的绿色丝带。此处泛指高官。
⑩棠棣：常用棠棣比喻如兄弟般的或子女般的亲密隶属关系。连阴：惠政，仁政。
⑪虎符：铜铸的虎形兵符，背有铭文。作为古代调兵遣将的信物。熊轼：指公卿和地方长官。
⑫夹河分守：典故出自《汉书·杜周传》："始周为庭史，有一马。及久任事，列三公，而两子夹河为郡守，家訾累巨万矣。"
⑬青云咫尺：不久即可高升。
⑭承明：此处指寿主二子不久将成为皇帝身边的高官。
⑮看彩衣争献：此处指子争相为母祝寿。彩衣：原指春秋时老莱子着彩衣娱亲。详见《艺文类聚·列女传》。
⑯兰羞：指香美的食品。玉酎（zhòu）：指复酿的醇美之酒。
⑰松椿比寿：祝寿之辞。松椿：松树、椿树，因树龄长，比喻高寿。

lady.
Congratulate her long longevity,
Wish her to be like a great pine,
Ever growing up, green and lofty.

蝶恋花①
上巳召亲族②

永夜恹恹③欢意少。
空梦长安④，
认取长安道。
为报今年春色好，
花光月影宜相照。

随意杯盘虽草草⑤。
酒美梅酸⑥，
恰称人怀抱。
醉里插花花莫笑，
可怜春似人将老。

Butterflies Fallen in Love with Flowers

Weak and weary through illness, I felt joyous a little.
At long night I dreamed of Chang'an Capital,
I know the long road to lead to my final goal.
In order to report this spring as a good view,
Flowery light should shine with the moon's shadow.

The dishes at will were fast cooked well.
Both drinks and fruits are so tasteful,
To satisfy the delicious need of the people.
Don't laugh at me as a tipsy person,
I'd like to insert a flower in hair-bun,
Flowery spring also will grow elder like a person.

【译注】

①蝶恋花：原唐教坊曲名，后用为词牌名。
②上巳：节日名。秦汉时，以阴历三月上旬巳日为“上巳”。魏晋以后改为阴历三月三日。
③永夜：长夜。恹恹（yān yān）：精神不振貌。
④长安：原为汉唐故都，这里代指北宋都城汴京。
⑤杯盘：指酒食。草草：简单粗糙。
⑥梅酸：代指菜肴可口。梅是古代所必需的调味品。

武陵春

风住尘香花已尽，
日晚倦梳头。
物是人非事事休，
欲语泪先流。

闻说双溪①春尚好，
也拟泛轻舟。
只恐双溪舴艋②舟，
载不动、许多愁。

Fairyland Spring

The wind was to rest,
With no fragrance in air dust,
And flowers in exhaust,
It is late, I am tired to have hair comb.
The thing is still the same thing,
But the changeable man is not exactly the same,
I'd like to talk to the man,
I cannot help but shedding tears time and again.

It was told Double-Brook spring is wonderful,
How I wish to have a light boat paddle.
Only I am afraid the riverboat too small,
Hardly to carry on my too much sorrow.

【译注】

①双溪：水名，在浙江金华，婺江上游义乌溪和永康溪两水在此交汇，故名。是唐宋时有名的游览胜地。

②舴艋（zé měng）：小船。

声声慢

寻寻觅觅①，
冷冷清清，
凄凄惨惨戚戚②。
乍暖还寒③时候，
最难将息④。
三杯两盏淡酒，
怎敌他、晓来风急⑤？
雁过也，
正伤心，
却是旧时相识。

满地黄花堆积，
憔悴损⑥，如今有谁堪摘？
守著窗儿，独自怎生得黑？
梧桐更兼细雨⑦，
到黄昏、点点滴滴。
这次第，怎一个、愁字了得⑧！

【译注】

①寻寻觅觅：述说想把失去的珍贵的一切找回来，又觉得非常迷茫、失落、空虚、怅惘。
②凄凄惨惨戚戚：忧愁苦闷。
③乍暖还寒：秋天忽然从暖转为寒冷。
④息：旧时方言，指欲休养调理。
⑤敌他：对付，抵挡。晓来：一本作"晚来"。（俞

Sounds Go Slow

I am to seek, seek and look for what I think,
I feel cold, lonely, so sad and so tragic,
To be sorrowful, unhappy and lovesick.
It's getting abruptly warm, still cold,
Keeping fit for me is difficult.
Two or three cups of soft wine,
Could stop dawn wind in cry?
The flying wild geese in a line,
As my old friends in the sky,
Being sad, I'm heartbroken with a sigh.

The ground full of flowers in yellow,
The withered were wan and sallow,
Who would like to pick?
I had to guard my window,
How lonely did I stay after dark?
The parasol-tree leaves clicked by the drizzle,
Drop-by-drop at dusk,
Such a series of rhythm click,
Could be generalized just by a word "sorrow"?

平伯《唐宋词选释》："晓来"，各本多作"晚来"，殆因下文"黄昏"云云。其实词写一整天，非一晚的事。若云"晚来风急"，则反而重复。）

⑥损：表示程度极高。

⑦梧桐更兼细雨：有读过白居易《长恨歌》"秋雨梧桐叶落时"诗句的痕迹。

⑧这次第：这光景、这情形。怎一个、愁字了得：一个"愁"字怎么能概括得尽呢？

点绛唇

寂寞深闺①，
柔肠一寸愁千缕。
惜春春去，
几点催花雨。

倚遍阑干，
只是无情绪。
人何处，
连天芳草，
望断归来路。

Beautify Lips by Crimson

My deep boudoir is lonely,
One piece of my heart broken,
1000-piece sorrows remain.
I have no way to keep spring to stay,
Raindrops promote flowers to fall easily.

It's the balustrade I am leaning upon,
I'm in no good spirits but depression.
Where is my man?
Fragrant grass approach heaven dome,
My eyes failed to see his way home.

【译注】

①闺：过去妇女居住的内室。

减字木兰花[1]

卖花担上，
买得一枝春欲放[2]。
泪染轻匀[3]，
犹带彤霞晓露痕。

怕郎猜道，
奴面不如花面好。
云鬓斜簪，
徒要教郎比并看[4]。

The Shortened Tune-Pattern of Magnolia Flower

Plum blossoms in a pole-basket on sale,
A fresh flower bought as spring's first symbol.
My tears lightly and evenly fall,
As if rolling with rosy clouds and dews still on the petal.

I am afraid my darling will know,
My look not better than the flowery look.
My thick hair inserted with a hairpin oblique,
I had no way to let my darling sure,
My look prettier than the blooming flower.

【译注】

①减字木兰花：词牌名。减字：指对某词调在音乐上减缩乐句或节奏，在歌词上减少字句，从而构成新调。

②买得一枝春欲放：此指买得一支将要开放的梅花。

③泪：指形似眼泪的晶莹露珠。轻匀：轻盈匀称。

④徒：只，但。比并：一并对比。

摊破浣溪沙[1]

揉破黄金万点轻，
剪成碧玉叶层层。
风度精神如彦辅[2]，
太[3]鲜明。

梅蕊重重何俗甚[4]，
丁香千结苦粗生[5]。
熏透[6]愁人千里梦，
却无情。

【译注】

①摊破浣溪沙：词牌名，又名《添字浣溪沙》。
②彦辅：西晋人，是当时名士，姓乐名广，字彦辅。《晋书·乐广传》谓广“性冲约，有远识，寡嗜欲，与物无竞……”，这里是以神姿朗彻的名士风度比拟桂花品格的清朗脱俗。
③太：一作“大”。
④何俗甚：俗不可耐。
⑤丁香千结：语出毛文锡《更漏子》词：“庭下丁香千结。”丁香千结应当是指丁香花花瓣重生。苦粗生：太粗。
⑥熏透：即被桂花香熏醒。

Expanded Washing Brook Sand

The myriad sweet osmanthus flowers,
Look like light soft golden papers,
They were cut into small pieces, layer by layer.
Their style was similar with Yan Fu[1] speaker,
As a versatile scholar, he was too wiser.

Comparatively, plum blossoms are more vulgar than the sweet osmanthus flower,
Thousands of cloves smell bitter,
Their smell fumigated sad personnel to awaken.
And a 1000-mile of dream broken,
But no affection!

【Annotation】

① Yan Fu: He was a famous scholar in the West Jin Dynasty, China (265 ~ 317).

摊破浣溪沙

病起萧萧两鬓华，
卧看残月上窗纱。
豆蔻连梢煎熟水，
莫分茶[1]。

枕上诗书闲处好，
门前风景雨来佳。
终日向人多酝藉[2]，
木犀[3]花。

Expanded Washing Brook Sand

My black hairs turn silver-grey after healthy recovery,
Lying on bed, I look up at the moon staring at screen.
The nutmeg was boiled into herb soup-medicine,
That's no share for others as I entertained the tea.

I read a poem freely while leaning upon my pillow,
Looking at the drizzle outside the door or window.
All day long, the mild drizzle let me comfort,
The sweet osmanthus-flower, sweet!

【译注】

①分茶：大约始于北宋初年。“分茶”就是烹茶、煎茶，是宋代流行的一种“茶道”。《剑南诗稿校注》卷十二《疏山东堂昼眠》下释分茶曰：“分茶，宋人泡茶之一种方法，即以开水注入茶碗之技艺。”

②酝藉：宽和有涵容。

③木犀：即木樨，系桂花的学名。

瑞鹧鸪[1]
双银杏

风韵雍容未甚都[2]，
尊前甘橘可为奴[3]。
谁怜流落江湖上，
玉骨冷肌未肯枯。

谁教并蒂连枝摘，
醉后明皇倚太真[4]。
居士擘开真有意，
要吟风味两家新[5]。

【译注】

①本作品以靖康之乱后金兵南渡为背景，写了李清照与丈夫赵明诚一起离乡背井、避乱南方的颠沛愁怀。《济南名士丛书·李清照全集评注》（济南出版社 1990 年 12 月出版）认为此诗前后押两韵部，其中间四句，既不对仗，而且上下阕衔接处，亦不黏连，实为两首绝句，误抄一起，《花草粹编》编者遽加《瑞鹧鸪》名，并妄题为“双银杏”。

②甚都：美好，雍容闲雅。

③甘橘可为奴：甘橘别称木奴（详见《三国志·吴书·孙休传》注引《襄阳记》）。

④太真：指杨玉环。

⑤“居士……”句：指李清照本人，易安居士把银杏壳掰开，夫妻一人一颗，情真意切。

A Pair of Auspicious Partridges
Double Ginkgoes

Ginkgo is not everything perfect but style graceful,
In comparison with orange, her fruit look general.
All over the world, who will sympathize in her style?
Her jade-like muscle and cold bone made her firm tall.

Picking such a pair of ginkgo like this, who told?
One twig of ginkgo links another twig of ginkgo.
As if Tang Minghuang and his concubine hold,
Drunk later, the emperor leaned upon her body.
A pair of ginkgoes nut broken but kept one pedigree,
One lyric love style remained in their uneasy family.

庆清朝慢

禁幄低张，
彤栏巧护，
就中独占残春。
容华淡伫[①]，
绰约[②]俱见天真。
待得群花过后，
一番风露晓妆新。
妖娆艳态，
妒风笑月，
长殢东君[③]。

东城边，
南陌上，
正日烘池馆，
竞走香轮。
绮筵[④]散日，
谁人可继芳尘。
更好明光宫殿，
几枝先近日边匀。
金尊倒，
拚了尽烛，
不管黄昏。

Slow Tune of Clear Morning Auspiciousness

The private tent set up a low screen to the sunshine,
The red veranda prevented flowers from light,
Flowers occupied all the spring residual sight.
They all were pink and luxurious to stand still,
Their tender faces looked naive and graceful.
After more and more blooming flowers faded away,
Peonies made new makeup by dews rolling freely.
Being enchanting was their fairy gesture's charm,
They were jealousy of breeze, smiling at the moon,
Girdling flowery Goddess to show the lovely tone.

Over the wall's east side and the southern lane,
The sun was drying the water-pavilion,
As the flowery-traveling cart wheels run.
After sharing a sumptuous feast,
Which flower will go fragrant?
Still better and brighter is the palace scene,
A few twigs of blossoms evenly look at the sun.

【译注】
①伫（zhù）：伫立，挺立。

The gold cup of wine is dry,
Stop the candle light,
Be regardless of the twilight.

②绰约：同婥约，又作淖约，指姿态柔美。

③殢（tì）：滞留。《东君》是先秦时期屈原所作，全名《九歌·东君》。相传该诗是为祭祀日神。（本词中也可理解为向阳开的花神或司美女神。）

④绮筵（qǐ yán）：华丽丰盛的筵席。

失调名

条脱闲揎①系五丝。

The Tune-Pattern Lost

Roll up sleeves to girdle around my wrist,
By the five kinds of silk thread-knitted belt.

【译注】
①揎（xuān）：将袖子露出手臂。

失调名

元旦①

瑞脑②烟残，
沉香③火冷。

【译注】

①这是李清照写与沉香相关的一首题为《元旦》的词中的一句，其调名已失。宋代陈元靓撰《岁时广记》（卷四十）有记载："李易安《元旦》词云:'瑞脑烟残,沉香火冷。'"(李清照号易安居士）该书同时引用了欧阳修写与沉香相关的两行诗："隋宫守夜沉香火，楚俗驱神爆竹声。"

②瑞脑：又称龙脑香、冰片，是龙脑香树树脂的结晶体，天然龙脑多形成于树干的裂缝中。称之为"龙脑"，以示其珍贵。

③沉香：名贵的木质香料。

The Tune-Pattern Lost

New Year's Eve①

The eagle-wood's residual smoke was to scatter,
Its burning fire was getting colder and colder.

【Annotation】

① This residual sentence was from Li Qingzhao's one of Chinese ci-poem entitled *New Year's* Eve but its tune pattern has been lost, and the whole original text could not be found, which was about the fragrant wood—the remaining sentence like this——

The eagle-wood's residual smoke was to scatter,
Its burning fire was getting colder and colder.

—quoted from the Song Dynasty scholar Chen Yuan Liang's monograph *Widely-recorded annotation on yearly seasonal changes* (volume forty).

The book also cited the Song Dynasty poet Ouyang Xiu 's two lines of poetry related to the fragrant wood:

At Sui harem vigil, fragrant wood burning kept on,
Chu-king appreciated to make fireworks last long.

Widely-recorded annotation on yearly seasonal changes also cited another classic section to praise Tang's heyday—During the Tang Dynasty, Emperor Li Shimin's period was called heyday. At that time, all over China had been peaceful for a long time. On New Year's Eve, he let the harem make large-scale decorative furnishings with bright candles, playing the music.

In order to entertain the former queen Xiaohou who

said: “The Sui-dynasty emperor was extravagant on each New Year’s Eve. In front of the harem with all the chambers, dozens of fragrant woods were burnt. Each hill nearby was to burn out a lot of fragrant woods transported by dozens of carts. A kind of easy-burnt fragrant woods would be added if the flame was weak. The flame would rise up for several meters high, the fragrant smell would go with the wind for more than ten miles. More than 200-cart of fragrant woods and more than 200 Chinese-dans of Jiajian-fragrant materials would be used. (dan, a unit of dry measure for grain, approximately 150 kg) .” Although Emperor Li Shimin said it’s too extravagant, still he thought that’s wonderful.

怨王孙

梦断漏悄，愁浓酒恼。
宝枕生寒，翠屏向晓。
门外谁扫残红？夜来风。

玉箫声断人何处？
春又去，忍把归期负。
此情此恨，
此际拟托行云，
问东君[1]。

Lyrics for King-Posterity

My dream was broken, the water-timer, tick by tick,
Too much wine accumulated my sorrows thick.
The precious pillow was getting colder,
The green screen reflected the daybreak.
Outside the door, who swept red residual leaves?
That's the night breeze.

The jade flute stopped playing, where was the man?
Spring was gone again,
The handsome guy was bearable to cancel our reunion.
It's my hatred and affection,
That would ask floating clouds to tell Sun God what I mean.

【注释】
①东君：指代太阳神或司春之神、司美之神等。

怨王孙

帝里[1]春晚，重门深院。
草绿阶前，暮天雁断。
楼上远信谁[2]传？恨绵绵[3]。

多情自是多沾惹[4]，难拚舍[5]，
又是寒食也。
秋千巷陌[6]，人静皎月初斜，
浸梨花[7]。

Lyrics for King-Posterity

In the capital city, spring came late,
The deep yard locked by an inner gate.
In front of door steps, grass turned green,
The wild geese vanished in the twilight heaven.
Who will deliver my letter afar from my pavilion?
My message's full of my lovesick pain.

My self feelings would attract the affectionate,
But hardly give up my sweet heart,
On the Cold Food Festival date.
The swing hung in the lane roadside,
There's no noisy player outside.
The slanting moon still kept clear and bright,
All of flowery pears immersed by the moonlight.

【注释】：
①帝里：指京城。
②谁：《古今诗余醉》题作"难"。
③绵绵：接连不断。
④沾惹：招引。
⑤拚舍：舍弃，屏除。
⑥巷陌：街道。
⑦浸梨花：月光像水一样浸透了梨花，犹言梨花沐浴在月光里。

生查子①

年年玉镜台，梅蕊宫妆②困。
今岁不归来，怕见江南信③。

酒从别后疏，泪向愁中尽。
遥想楚云④深，人远天涯近。

Unripe Hawthorn

Year by year, the jade-mirror table for the beautiful,
Few plum pistils can hardly let palace girls graceful.
This year the young man was not returning home,
The girl was afraid to receive his letter afar in sorrow.

She has seldom drunk wine since being apart,
Her shedding tears fell into her broken heart.
She imagined lofty clouds afar in the sky,
As if seeing her darling coming nearby.

【译注】

①此词更多倾向于朱淑真所作，曾列宋金十大名曲之八。

②梅蕊宫妆：喻女子华美妆饰，或喻梅花。

③江南信：泛指远方的令人忧伤的信息。

④楚云：楚天之云或比喻女子秀美的发髻。

丑奴儿

晚来一阵风兼雨，洗尽炎光。
理罢笙簧，却对菱花淡淡妆。

绛绡缕薄冰肌莹①，雪腻酥香。
笑语檀郎②，今夜纱厨③枕簟凉。

Comic Clown

A gust of wind and a gust of rain at late twilight,
Sweep and wash off all the burning hot light.
Facing her mirror, she combed with thin makeup,
And then playing flute.

My crimson silk fabric sleeping coat, put over her muscle to be transparent,
Her snow-white skin smelling fragrant.
Her darling whispered with a smiling show,
The cool night shrouded bamboo mat and pillow.

【译注】

①绛绡缕薄冰肌莹：绛红薄绡的透明睡衣朦朦胧胧，雪白的肌肤若隐若现。绡：丝织品。

②檀郎：指夫君。

③纱厨：指张在床上的帐子。

点绛唇

蹴[1]罢秋千，起来慵整[2]纤纤手。
露浓花瘦，薄汗轻衣透。

见客入来[3]，袜刬[4]金钗溜。
和羞走。
倚门回首，却把青梅嗅。

【译注】

①蹴（cù）：踩，踏。这里指荡（秋千）。

②慵整：懒洋洋地收拾。

③见客入来：一作“见有人来”。

④袜刬（chǎn）：未穿鞋子，只穿着袜子行走。

Beautify Lips by Crimson

Let feet touch ground stop the swing,
Leave it off to have tender hands releasing.
The rolling dews thick, the blooming flowers few,
My thin sweat immersed my inner shirt through.

Seeing guests come in,
I put off shoes but socks put on, my hairpin slipping down.
In shy manners, I walk along,
Looking back, I lean upon the gate,
To sniff the plum blossom fragrant.

浪淘沙

帘外五更[①]风，吹梦无踪。
画楼重上与谁同？
记得玉钗斜拨火，宝篆成空[②]。

回首紫金峰，雨润烟浓。
一江春浪醉醒中。
留得罗襟前日泪，弹与征鸿。

【译注】

①五更：旧时自黄昏至拂晓一夜间，分为甲、乙、丙、丁、戊五段，谓之“五更”。此处指第五更，即凌晨3—5点，天将明时。

②宝篆成空：器之尊者，谓“宝”；文之统者，谓“篆”。“宝篆”是古人焚香的美称。形容沉香焚时烟如篆状，如古老篆体字一般地消散在空中，好似龙凤舞动，将“香”的形状比作了“宝篆”，形、神、意恰到好处。

Billows Cleaning Out Sands

It's the daybreak wind outside the curtain,
To blow my dream broken.
Who will accompany me?
As I go upstairs to the pavilion.
I recall my hairpin used to adjust incenses burning,
Incense ashes remained but left nothing.

Looking back the Violet-Gold peak,
I see the rain-moistening fog thick.
A river of spring waves let me drunk and awake.
The front part of my garment, romantic tears moisten,
As if throwing at the flying wild geese in the heaven.

殢[1]人娇

玉瘦[2]香浓，檀深[3]雪散，
今年恨、探梅又晚。
江楼楚馆[4]，云闲水远。
清昼永，凭阑翠帘低卷。

坐上客来，尊前酒满，
歌声共、水流云断。
南枝[5]可插，更[6]须频剪。
莫待西楼，数声羌管[7]。

【译注】

①殢（tì）：（1）滞留：“进乏梯媒退又难，强随豪贵殢长安。”（2）纠缠：“要索新词，殢人含笑立尊前。”（3）困于，沉溺于：“犹自殢于酒色而不思讨贼。”

②玉瘦：指梅花瘦小。

③檀深：指（梅花）深红色。

④江楼楚馆：此词可能是借鉴于古文“青楼楚馆”（泛指歌舞场所或妓院）的结构并取其部分内涵。通常指远行的爱侣所居之处。江楼：临江的楼。

⑤南枝：向阳的梅枝。

⑥更：《梅苑》作“便”。（《梅苑》是南宋时期的一本词选）

⑦西楼：借指思念者的居所。羌管：即羌笛，古代羌族的一种乐器。

The Perplexing Maiden Is Gentle

Jade-like plum blossoms sparse with thick sweet smell,
Deeply red-white flowers bloom till melting of snow,
This year, it is regretfully late to look at them to go.
Upon the pavilion, I can see clouds free, water flow.
The whole clear day seemed to be long,
The late green curtain kept to half roll down.

Guests came in, sitting side by side,
Their cups were full of wine,
Pals sang together, as if stream running on,
and soon drifting clouds broken down.
You might decorate sunny-side blooming twigs for you,
It is necessary to pick up much more the beautiful.
Do not wait for your lovesick hall,
but listening to Qiangdi flute's call.

青玉案[1]

征鞍不见邯郸路，莫便匆匆归去。
秋风萧条何以度？明窗小酌，
暗灯清话，最好留连处。

相逢各自伤迟暮，独把新词诵奇句。
盐絮[2]家风人所许。
如今憔悴，但余双泪，一似黄梅雨[3]。

Bluish Jade Plate

On the warring saddle, Handan-road was invisible,
Do not hurry up to return your city capital.
Why the rustling autumn wind was to blow?
Drinking a little, I faced the bright window.
Under a dark lantern, I talked to no person,
At the best place to hide my inner emotion.

It's much late to meet each other in gloom,
Still reciting my new lyric as an odd poem.
Stubbornly a literary style shrouded our home.
Now how haggard I am,
My tears full in my double eyes,
As if lingering rainy season of plum.

【译注】

①青玉案：词牌名，取于东汉张衡《四愁诗》"美人赠我锦绣段，何以报之青玉案"一句。写此词时李清照已经52岁，从济南南下杭州的这一年一直寄住弟弟李远家中。离别与重逢之间，多少滋味涌上心头。于是有了这一首《青玉案》。

②盐絮：谢安侄女道韫，才思敏捷，尝居家遇雪，安曰："何所似也？"安兄子朗曰："散盐空中差可拟。"道韫曰："未若柳絮因风起。"谢安十分赞赏。后因以"盐絮"指美好的诗句或以指诗才。

③黄梅雨：初夏时节，江南梅子成熟，故称"梅雨"或"黄梅雨"。又因此时温度高、湿度大、风速小、光照奇缺，器物易发霉，所以又称"霉雨"。

浣溪沙

髻子伤春慵①更梳，
晚风庭院落梅初。
淡云来往月疏疏。

玉鸭熏炉闲瑞脑②，
朱樱斗帐掩流苏③。
通犀④还解辟寒无？

Washing Brook Sand

In lovesick's pring, I'm weary to comb hair-bun carefully,
The breeze blows plum blossoms falling down early.
Thin clouds floating back and forth were sparse.

Jade duck-shaped censer's incenses burnt of spices,
The bed-curtain was beautified with the red tassel.
Also magic rhinoceros horn could stop the cold gale.

【译注】

①慵：《历代名媛诗词》作“恼”。

②玉鸭熏炉：玉制的点燃熏香的鸭形香炉。熏炉有麒麟、狮子、鸭子等不同形状；质料也有金、铜、铁、玉、瓷等不同。瑞脑：一种香料，或称龙脑香。

③朱樱斗帐：覆斗形的帐子。流苏：帐子下垂的穗儿，一般用五色羽毛或彩线盘结而成。

④通犀：五代王仁裕《开元天宝遗事》记载过犀角能避寒气的史料——“辟寒犀”：“开元二年冬至，交趾国进犀一株，色黄似金。使者请以金盘置于殿中，温温然有暖气袭人。上问其故。使对曰：‘此避寒犀也。’”

浪淘沙

素约小腰身[1]，不奈伤春。
疏梅影下晚妆新。
袅袅娉娉何样似[2]，一缕轻云。

歌巧动朱唇，字字娇嗔[3]。
桃花深径一通津。
怅望瑶台清夜月，还送归轮。

Billows Cleaning Out Sands

Her waist was so slender, so graceful,
Not to hurt spring to be beautiful.
The sparse plum blossoms' shadow,
Sheltered her late makeup freshly to show.
What could be compared with her slim gesture?
Only a flying cloud was so slim, so slender.

A pleasant song floated from crimson lips' corner,
Each word showed her pettishly lovely manner.
A long peach blossom path approached Milky Way.
The maiden looked for the moon melancholy,
To wait for her sailing love ship back in hurry.

【译注】

①素约小腰身：苗条身材。

②袅袅：细长柔美的样子。形容女子苗条俊美，体态轻盈。唐杜牧《赠别二首》："娉娉袅袅十三余，豆蔻梢头二月初。"娉娉（pīng pīng）：秀美的样子。

③娇嗔（chēn）：佯装生气的娇态。

鹧鸪天①

枝上流莺和泪闻，
新啼痕间旧啼痕。
一春鱼鸟②无消息，
千里关山劳梦魂。

无一语，对芳尊③。
安排④肠断到黄昏。
甫能⑤炙得灯儿了，
雨打梨花深闭门。

The Partridge Sky

Tears dropping, I heard of the nightingale singing in the tree,
The new song afar reminded of my past good memory.
No spring news was heard of flying birds or swimming fish,
I dreamed of a 1000-mile mountain with an arch-pass.

Saying nothing to hold a cup of sweet wine,
The heartbroken reunion lasted to twilight.
Just now the oil-lamp turned dry,
The door shut up, no raindrops stop,
Falling on pear blossoms' top.

【题解】

此词创作时间未详，其作者也尚有争议。清代王鹏运四印斋本《漱玉词补遗》案语以为北宋词人秦观所作。汲古阁未刻词本《漱玉词》收此词，以为李清照所作。而《全宋词》归入无名氏的作品。

【译注】

①鹧鸪天：词牌名。调名取自唐人郑嵎诗“春游鸡鹿塞，家在鹧鸪天”。小令词调，又名“思佳客”“思越人”“剪朝霞”“骊歌一叠”等。

②鱼鸟：犹鱼雁。相传鸿雁、鲤鱼可以传递书信。

③芳尊：尊，通“樽”。精致的酒器或借指美酒。

④安排：听任自然的变化。

⑤甫能：宋时方言，刚才。

青玉案

一年春事都来几？
早过了、三之二。
绿暗红嫣浑可事①，绿杨庭院，
暖风帘幕，有个人憔悴。

买花载酒长安市，
又争似家山桃李②？
不枉③东风吹客泪，相思难表，
梦魂无据，惟有归来是。

Bluish Jade Plate

This spring, how many romantic stories happen?
Such a season so early began!
Its two-thirds period passed again.
Green willow shade and red plums everywhere vividly,
Green lofty poplars show the courtyard to be gloomy,
The mild breeze warmed her bed-curtain,
She looked like a haggard maiden.

Alcohols and flowers sold in the capital,
Those were better than those at home.
Helpless to let down the east wind blow tears to fall,
There is no place I can put into my dreamy soul,
However, still I have a lonely road to go home.

【题解】

此词见于人民文学出版社《李清照集校注》（王仲闻），有学者认为是欧阳修之作。

【译注】

①嫣：指人容貌美好或花朵艳丽。浑：全。可事：小事，寻常之事。

②争似：怎像。家山：家乡的山，指故乡。

③不枉：不要冤枉，不怪。

失调名[1]

教[2]我甚情怀。

The Tune-Pattern Lost

My past love emotion,
Ever let me heartbroken.

【译注】

①《失调名》的作者是李清照，被选入《全宋词》，全篇无觅处，只残此一句，记载于《花草粹编》卷二朱秋娘《采桑子》词集句中。

②教：此处有“使、令、让”等字义。

卷二　诗

Part Two Poems

浯溪中兴颂诗和张文潜[1]（二首）

（其一）

五十年功[2]如电扫，
华清花柳咸阳草[3]。
五坊供奉斗鸡儿[4]，
酒肉堆中不知老。
胡兵[5]忽自天上来，
逆胡亦是奸雄才。
勤政楼[6]前走胡马，
珠翠踏尽香尘埃。
何为出战辄披靡[7]，
传置荔枝多马死[8]，
尧功舜德本如天，
安用区区纪文字。
著碑铭德[9]真陋哉，
乃令神鬼磨山崖。
子仪光弼不自猜[10]，
天心悔祸[11]人心开。
夏商有鉴[12]当深戒，
简策汗青[13]今具在。
君不见，当时张说最多机，
虽生已被姚崇卖[14]。

Follow after Wenqian Zhang's Rhymes The Mid-Tang Heyday Glorification Carved on Wu-Stream-Cliff

One

The fifty-year reign passed as a lightning moment,
The palace willows and blossoms still remained.
The five game-halls were used to play the cockfighting,
Except wine and pork, the aged emperor knew nothing.
The Hu-rebels suddenly jumped down from the sky,
Their top leader was a traitor and dirty spy.
To the imperial palace, Hu-knights marched on,
Its pearls and jade jewels were trampled down.
Why the emperor did not win the battle against the enemy?
As more military horses were died to transport litchi.
Ancient pioneer Yao-Shun's merits and virtues were so greater,
But he had never carved his glorification on

【译注】

①张文潜(1054—1114): 北宋诗人，名耒(lěi)，字文潜，苏轼门下“四学士”之一。

②五十年功：唐玄宗（李隆基）在位实际四十四年，“五十年”为大约数字。

③华清：华清宫，在陕西临潼骊山西北麓。咸阳：秦建都之地。

④五坊：据《新唐书·百官志》记载：“闲厩使押五坊以供时狩，一曰雕坊，二曰鹘坊，三曰鹞坊，四曰鹰坊，五曰狗坊。”后人指不务正业之人为“五坊小儿”。斗鸡儿：借指唐玄宗爱好斗鸡，玩物丧志。

⑤胡兵：指安禄山叛乱部队。安禄山、史思明皆为胡人。下句逆胡亦指安禄山、史思明。

⑥勤政楼：唐玄宗建，为唐明皇赐宴设酺之处。全称“勤政务本之楼”。

⑦披靡：溃败。

⑧传置荔枝：《新唐书·杨贵妃传》：“妃嗜荔枝，必欲生致之，乃置骑传送数千里，味未变，已至京师。”多马死：日夜兼程，骏马多有累死。

⑨著碑铭德：撰写碑文铭记功德。

⑩子仪：郭子仪，唐代名将，唐玄宗时，累迁朔方节度使，平安史之乱有功，封汾阳王。光弼：李光弼，唐代名将。平安史之乱有功，授天下兵纪都元帅，封淮郡王。不自猜：二人互不猜疑。

⑪天心悔祸：上天不欲重复其错误。

⑫夏商有鉴：一作“夏为殷鉴”。

⑬简策汗青：代指史册。（古时将竹简在火上烤干，炙烤时竹简出水如汗一般，故曰汗青。）

⑭“君不见”三句：诸位不见那，当时的张说最是心机为多。张说、姚崇：二人均为唐玄宗时宰相。

stone forever.

An inscription on stone to praise somebody is ugly,

That will make the ghost milling cliff silently.

Two generals were being distrusted by the “heaven-son”,

The emperor regretted his wrong doing with suspicion.

Be careful to take warning from Xia-Shang Dynasty,

Their bamboo slips were written of lessons in history.

Do you know Prime Minister Zhang was good in strategy?

But betrayed by another Prime Minister Yao adversary.

浯溪中兴颂诗和张文潜（二首）

（其二）

君不见，
惊人废兴传天宝①，
中兴碑上今生草。
不知负国有奸雄，
但说成功尊国老②。
谁令妃子③天上来，
虢、秦、韩国④皆天才。
花桑羯鼓玉方响⑤，
春风不敢生尘埃⑥。
姓名谁复知安史，
健儿猛将安眠死。
去天尺五抱瓮峰⑦，
峰头凿出开元字。
时移势去真可哀，
奸人心丑⑧深如崖。
西蜀万里尚能反⑨，
南内⑩一闭何时开。
可怜孝德如天大，
反使将军称好在⑪。
呜呼，奴辈乃不能道："辅国用事张后尊⑫。"
乃能念："春荠长安作斤卖⑬。"

Follow after Wenqian Zhang's Rhymes The Mid-Tang Heyday Glorification Carved on Wu-Stream-Cliff

Two

Do you see Tang Minghuang lost his heyday during his reign?
Now his tomb with glorification monument grass in green.
He had no idea of the traitors to betray his country,
But believed they obeyed the old generals earnestly.
Who made the concubine come from the heaven?
Her each sister was granted as a kingdom's queen.
The Jie-minority drum accompanied instrumental music,
The spring winds do not dare to have all the dust work.
Who would like to recall the two traitors An and Shi?
For valiant generals and strong soldiers fought to death.
It's just five-feet to reach the sky from Hold-Urn Peak,
On the top, at character Kaiyuan-reign one

may look.
As time goes on, it's really sad to turn a weak country,
Traitors' ugly inner world was as deep as a cliff valley.
It's possible to escape 10000s of miles to West-Shu region,
When the gate of South-Inside palace would be open again?
The pitiful filial piety was considered to be so great,
That the military general was benefited yet.
Alas, Prime Minister Li's or Queen Zhang's affairs,
Too shy to talk about.
Only the people could call loudly on sale,
Of spring mustard in Chang'an's market.

【译注】
①天宝：唐玄宗年号。
②国老：告老退休的卿大夫。此指郭子仪、李光弼等平息安史之乱的功臣。
③妃子：指杨贵妃。
④虢、秦、韩国：杨贵妃三姊分封之地。
⑤羯鼓：乐器，以山桑木制成。方响：乐器。
⑥“春风”句：指明皇与贵妃击鼓作乐时，使得春风也不敢吹起尘埃。
⑦去天尺五：此极言其高。抱瓮峰：即华山瓮肚峰。
⑧奸人心丑：奸人，奸诈之人，此指李辅国等。丑，险恶。
⑨反：同“返”。
⑩南内：长安有大内、西内、南内三宫，南内原本是唐玄宗听政处。安史之乱平息后，玄宗回到长安，肃宗信用李辅国，迁玄宗于西内，以“南内一闭”暗指玄宗失位。
⑪将军：指高力士，天宝七年加封至骠骑大将军。称好在：说好否。
⑫辅国用事：辅国即李辅国，玄宗时为阉奴，得肃宗信任，权势日益显赫。用事，当权。张后：肃宗皇后，与李辅国勾结专权，后为李辅国所杀。

⑬春荠长安作斤卖：《旧唐书·高力士传》载，高力士被流放到贵州时，见当地人不知道吃荠菜，曾写诗一首自喻身世变迁：“两京秤斤卖，五溪无人采。夷夏虽有殊，气味应不改。”

【题解】

这两首诗是李清照对张耒的诗《读中兴颂碑》一诗的酬和。李清照的和诗深刻分析了唐朝之所以会发生安史之乱和唐王朝军队一败涂地的原因，其诗不独将腐化昏聩的唐明皇和诸般谄媚误国的佞臣一同作了鞭挞，总结历史的教训，且揭示了北宋末年腐败的朝政、君主荒淫无能、臣僚尔虞我诈。诗人借古喻今，对当权者予以劝戒，表现了诗人忧国忧民的伟大胸怀。

上枢密韩公诗

（并序）

绍兴癸丑[①]五月，枢密韩公、工部尚书胡公使虏[②]，通两宫也[③]。有易安室者[④]，父祖皆出韩公门下[⑤]，今家世沦替[⑥]，子姓[⑦]寒微，不敢望公之车尘[⑧]。又贫病，但神明[⑨]未衰落。见此大号令，不能忘言，作古、律诗各一章，以寄区区之意，以待采诗者云。

【译注】

①绍兴：南宋高宗年号。癸丑：即绍兴三年（1133 年）。

②胡公：即胡松年，时任工部侍郎，李清照以尚书称之以示敬意。使：出使。虏：金国鄙称。

③通：通问、问候。两宫：指被金人掳去的宋徽宗和宋钦宗。

④易安室者：李清照自称。

⑤父祖皆出韩公门下：韩公，指韩肖胄曾祖韩琦，安阳人。韩琦历任仁宗、英宗、神宗三朝宰相。李清照的祖父和父亲（李格非）皆曾为韩琦荐引，故曰出韩公门下。

⑥家世沦替：指家世业沦落不振。

⑦子姓：子孙，这里指李氏后人。

⑧不敢望公之车尘：这里是谦语。意思是指今韩肖胄地位显赫，已与之悬殊，不敢登门拜见。

⑨神明：精神、意识。

Preface

In May, 1133, the Song-Dynasty Diplomat Han Xiaozhou, and Deputy Diplomat Hu Songnian (of the Engineering Ministry) were sent to see the Song's two emperors captured by the Jin's regime.

Li Yi'an used as my literary name. My father or forefathers all had good relationship with imperial high official Han's family one generation after another.

Nowadays, my family had not been so prosperous but to be getting weaker and poorer; we dare not to follow after them to recall our past reputation.

Despite of the poor, still we are rich and intelligent in spirit. Therefore, seeing the Song's decree to send Diplomat Han, I am unable to forget writing two poems to show my concern for Diplomat Han's great mission to the Jin Regime, one of my poems is classical, and the other is a rhythmically metrical poem.

【其一】

三年夏六月，天子视朝久。
凝旒望南云[1]，垂衣思北狩[2]。
如闻帝若曰，岳牧与群后[3]。
贤宁无半千[4]，运已遇阳九[5]。
勿勒燕然铭[6]，勿种金城柳[7]。
岂无纯孝臣[8]，识此霜露悲[9]。
何必羹舍肉[10]，便可车载脂[11]。
土地非所惜，玉帛如尘泥。
谁当可将命[12]，币[13]厚辞益卑。

【译注】

①凝旒（níng liú）：指天子冕穗一动不动，形容庄重严肃。旒：古代帝王之冕前后所悬垂的玉穗。《礼记·玉藻》：“天子玉藻，十有二旒，前后邃延。”南云：南天之云。天子面南而坐，故所望为南云。

②垂衣：言天下太平而无为。《周易·系辞》：“黄帝、尧、舜垂衣裳而天下治，盖取诸乾坤。”北狩：狩，本意为狩猎，引申为出巡。宋徽、钦二宗被掳北去，不敢明言，托词出巡，故曰北狩。

③岳牧：泛指朝廷百官。岳：尧帝时以羲和的四子分掌四岳诸侯。牧：一州之长为牧。群后：各位诸侯，泛指百官。

④半千：即员半千。《新唐书·员半千传》：“半千始名余庆，生而孤，为从父鞠爱。羁通书史。

Two Poems Written to the Song Diplomat Han Xiaozhou

One

It's June in summer of Emperor Zhao Gou's reign,
The palace had been long cared by the heaven's son.
He looked up at the southern cloud through the tassel,
Worrying of Song's former monarch captured by Jin rival.
As if the Song emperor were affectionately saying,
To sympathize his dukes or princes in weeping.
The peaceful reign had not lasted half a century,
A great disaster already fell on the country.
Do not carve an inscription on Yanran Mountain,
Do not plant the Gold-City willow for glorification.
Isn't there any truly loyal official,
To see the sad frosty dews fall?
No need to contribute your drink and pork,
If you let warring carts wheel fast and quick.
You never mind of losing the territory,

客晋州，州举童子，房玄龄异之。对诏高第，已能讲《易》《老子》。长与何彦光同事王义方。以迈秀见赏。义方常曰：'五百载一贤者生，子宜当之。'因改今名。"泛指贤能的人。
⑤阳九：指岁月充满灾难。古称4617岁为一元，初入元106岁中，将逢灾岁九，为阳九（《汉书·律历志》）。晋刘琨《劝进表》："方今钟百王之季，当阳九之运。"故阳九为厄运。诗中以阳九代指"靖康之难"。
⑥勒：刻石。燕然铭：《后汉书·窦宪传》："窦宪、耿秉与北单于战于稽落山，大破之。虏众奔溃，单于遁走……宪、秉遂登燕然山，出塞三千余里，刻石勒功，纪汉威德，令班固作铭。"
⑦金城柳：用晋桓温北伐故事。《晋书·桓温传》："温自江陵北伐，行经金城，见少为琅邪时所种柳皆已十围，慨然曰：'木犹如此，人何以堪！'攀枝执条，泫然流涕。"
⑧纯孝臣：韩肖胄事母以孝闻，故称。
⑨霜露悲：指怀念父母之情。《礼记》："霜露既降，君子履之，必有凄怆之心，非其寒之谓也。春雨露既濡，君子履之，必有怵惕之心，如将见之。"
⑩羹（gēng）舍肉：《左传·隐公元年》："颍考叔为颍谷封人……公赐之食。食舍肉。公问之。对曰：'小人有母，皆尝小人之食矣，未尝君之羹，请以遗之。'公曰：'尔有母遗，繄我独无！'颍考叔曰：'敢问何谓也？'公语之故，且告之悔。对曰：'君何患焉？若阙地及泉，隧而相见，其谁曰不然？'公从之。"
⑪车载脂：用油脂涂车轴，以使其走得快一些。《诗经·卫风·泉水》："载脂载舝。"
⑫将命：奉命。
⑬币：此指贡献给金人的钱物。

The rival would not treasure your jade or silk.
Who should be to obey the contribution order?
More contribution to others meant to surrender.

四岳佥曰俞[14]，臣下帝所知。
中朝第一人[15]，春官有昌黎[16]。
身为百夫特[17]，行足万人师。
嘉祐与建中[18]，为政有皋夔[19]。
匈奴畏王商[20]，吐蕃尊子仪[21]。
夷狄[22]已破胆，将命公所宜。
公拜手稽首，受命白玉墀[23]。
曰臣敢辞难，此亦何等时。
家人安足谋[24]，妻子不必辞。
愿奉天地灵，愿奉宗庙威。
径持紫泥诏，直入黄龙城。
单于定稽颡[25]，侍子当来迎。
仁君方恃信，狂生休请缨。
或取犬马血，与结天日盟。

All the four-duke top leaders were appointed
decisively,
The ancient emperor had known all of them
affirmatively.
Li Kui should be considered as the first
diplomatic man,
In Spring Palace, Han Yu was in charge of
Rites Ministry.
As an elite, you outstood out of 100 talented
people,
Like a teacher, you could teach 10000 students
in all.
During the Jiayou-reign and the Jianzhong-
reign,
Still there's a typical Gaokui-like official man.
Wang Shang was so stalwart to terrify the Hun ,
General Guo Ziyi was really respected by the
Tibetan.
The best diplomat could complete the difficult
mission,
The barbarians were so scared as if
gallbladders broken.
For they got best envoys' imperial proper
instruction,
The diplomat bent over to make a polite show,
To convey an imperial note at door steps of
marble.
As an official, he won't dare to fear any
difficulty,
It's an urgent time to contribute his capability.

【译注】

⑭四岳：四方诸侯之长。《尚书·尧典》：“帝曰：咨，四岳。”注：“四岳即羲和之四子，分掌四岳之诸侯，故称焉。”佥（qiān）：都。俞：表示答应的语气词。

⑮中朝第一人：指唐人李揆。李揆为唐肃宗时宰相，肃宗称其“门第人物、文学皆当世第一”。后李揆奉命出使外藩，外藩酋长问他：“闻唐有第一人李揆，公是否？”李揆恐被拘，故意道：“非也。他那个李揆怎肯到此。”（见《新唐书·李揆传》）

⑯春官：《周礼·春官宗》：“乃立春官宗伯，使帅其属，而掌邦礼，以佐玉和邦国。”春官，相当于后世之礼部。昌黎：唐韩愈。韩愈曾追赠礼部尚书，此以韩愈代指韩肖胄。

⑰百夫特：杰出人物。《诗经·秦风·黄鸟》：

It’s good enough to say yes to family peace.
Do not too much care of wife’s family affairs.
May God have wise soul to let him intelligent!
May ancestors’ temple be full of mighty spirit!
The diplomat held imperial decree with jade red print seal,
Directly to enter Yellow Dragon City to hand it to Jin’s official.
The Jin-regime official knelt down to worship to the envoy,
The waiter went out of palace to greet him politely.
The benevolent diplomat’s prestige based on his loyalty.
The reckless could not go abroad to work with other country.
The heaven-horse’s blood was used as an oath-ambition,
For building up a co-operation was like the heaven and sun.

“维此奄息，百夫之特。”郑注：“百夫之中最雄俊也。”

⑱嘉祐（jiā yòu）：宋仁宗赵祯年号。建中：即建中靖国，宋徽宗赵佶年号。

⑲皋夔（gāo kuí）：指贤臣。皋：虞舜时为狱官。夔：舜时乐正也。韩肖胄曾祖韩琦嘉祐年间曾任宰相，祖韩忠彦建中靖国年间为宰相。

⑳王商：汉成帝母王太后之弟，曾代匡衡为相。《汉书·王商传》：“为人多质有威重，长八尺余，身体鸿大，容貌甚过绝人。河平四年，单于来朝，引见白虎殿。丞相商坐未央廷中，单于前，拜谒商。商起，离席与言。单于仰视商貌，大畏之，迁延却退。天子闻而叹曰：此真汉相矣。”

㉑吐蕃尊子仪：据《新唐书·郭子仪传》记载：回纥、吐蕃入侵，郭子仪自率铠骑二千出入阵中。回纥怪问：“是谓谁？”报曰：“郭令公。”惊曰：“令公存乎？怀恩言天可汗弃天下，令公即世，中国无主，故我从以来。公今存，天可汗存乎？”报曰：“天子万寿。”回纥悟曰：“彼欺我乎！”

㉒夷狄（yí dí）：古时指边远地区少数民族。

㉓白玉墀（chí）：以白玉为阶，代指宫殿。

㉔家人安足谋：建炎以来系年要录：“肖胄母文安郡太夫人文氏闻肖。”

㉕稽颡（qǐ sǎng）：古代一种跪拜礼。

胡公清德人所难，
谋同德协心志安。
脱衣已被汉恩暖，
离歌不道易水寒。
皇天久阴后土湿，
雨势未回风势急。
车声辚辚马萧萧，
壮士懦夫俱感泣。
闾阎嫠妇[26]亦何知，
沥血投书干记室[27]。
夷虏从来性虎狼[28]，
不虞预备庸何伤[29]。
衷甲[30]昔时闻楚幕，
乘城前日记平凉[31]。
葵丘践土非荒城[32]，
勿轻谈士弃儒生[33]。
露布词成马犹倚[34]，
崤函关[35]出鸡未鸣。
巧匠何曾弃樗栎[36]，
刍荛之言[37]或有益。
不乞隋珠与和璧[38]，
只乞乡关新信息。
灵光虽在应萧萧[39]，
草中翁仲[40]今何若。
遗氓[41]岂尚种桑麻，
残虏如闻保城郭。
嫠家父祖生齐鲁，
位下名高人比数[42]。
当时稷下[43]纵谈时，
犹记人挥汗成雨[44]。

It's difficult to act as well as Envoy Hu in morality,
He cooperated with Deputy Envoy Han harmoniously.
Off clothes, they would feel warm from the Song's land,
When farewell, no need to sing a song Yi-River Cold.
Being long cloudy, the imperial land was wet,
The rainy situation lost, but the wind urgent.
Chariots rumble to roll, and horses neigh to gallop,
Both the heroic and the timid were excited to weep.
A poor widow knew a little bit of the diplomatic,
I wanted to write to the secretary in blood-ink.
Jin-barbarians were characterized as the wolf and tiger,
Necessary to prevent the ruthlessness from their nature.
Armors put on were ready to fight when warring flags visible,
Do not forget the past lesson how to climb up Pingliang's wall.
The two cities Kui and Jian should be given much regard,
Do not belittle a good speaker, but respect the Confucian scholar.
Scholar Yuan Hu could write an imperial

子孙南渡今几年，
飘零遂与流人[45]伍。
欲将血泪寄山河，
去洒东山一抔土[46]。

【译注】

㉖嫠（lí）妇：寡妇。

㉗沥血投书：沥血：指滴血。投书：递交书信。记室：古代官名，相当近代秘书。汉魏时始设。宋高承《事物纪原》："其官始见于魏武之世矣。宋用晋制，自明帝后，皇子帝虽非都督，亦置记室参军。则记室而为参军，晋制也。宋朝亦置于诸王府，曰某王府记室也。"

㉘夷虏（lǔ）：指金统治者。性虎狼：本性像虎狼般残暴。

㉙不虞预备：防范不测之事。《左传·文六年》："备预不虞。"庸何伤：有什么害处呢？

㉚衷甲：衷，同"中"。中甲，即将甲穿在衣服以内。《左传》记载，楚人欲于盟会时突袭晋，兵士皆将甲穿在衣服里面，使晋人不防备。

㉛乘城：登城。平凉：地名，在今甘肃省。《唐书·马越传》记载：唐贞元三年五月十五日，浑瑊与吐蕃相盟于平凉，吐蕃埋伏重兵突然袭击。

㉜葵丘：春秋时宋国地名，在今河南省。践土：春秋时郑国地名，在今河南省。晋文公曾于

decree on his horse-back,
Envoy Meng Shangjun could make roosters early report the daybreak.
A skillful carpenter never gave up poor wood,
The common people's speech might be good.
Do not be greedy to have the Sui-pearl and Heshi-jade,
But try to hear of new messages from the native land.
The Soul-light palace still remained with the wind soughing and sighing,
In grass, the tomb-way stone-carved guards or animals should be standing.
The former-dynasty adherents were to plant the mulberry,
The residual captives were told to defend the inner-city.
My ancestors were born in Qi-Lu kingdom territory,
Their position was low but reputation high in history.
In ancient city Jixia, scholars could freely talk about their own opinion,
Still with good memories, the people argued to sweat into the rain.
The later generations had wandered for several years in the southern land,
The people in exile were turning homeless far away from their native land.
They would like to dedicate to their own

此与齐、宋、郑、卫等国会盟。
㉝谈士：口才善辩之人。弃儒生：《汉书·郦生传》："沛公不好儒……未可以儒生说。"
㉞露布：即布告，此指军中报捷的文书。古时用兵获胜，上其功报于朝，谓之露布。马犹倚：《世说新语·文学》："桓宣武北征，袁虎时从，被责免官。会须露布文，唤袁倚马前令作，手不辍笔，俄得七纸，殊可观。东亭在侧，极叹其才，袁虎曰：'当令齿舌间得利。'"
㉟崤函关：亦称函谷关。
㊱樗栎（chū lì）：不成材之木。
㊲刍荛（chú ráo）之言：采薪者、捕鱼者之言，指地位低下的人说的话。
㊳隋珠：《淮南子·览冥训》："譬如隋侯之珠，和氏之璧，得之者富，失之者贫。"和璧：即和氏璧。
㊴灵光：汉鲁恭王殿名。萧萧：萧条状。
㊵翁仲：秦阮翁仲，南海人。身长一丈三尺，气质端勇，异于常人。始皇使率兵守临洮，声振匈奴，死后铸其铜像于咸阳宫司马门外。后人泛称坟墓或建筑物前后的石像为翁仲。
㊶遗氓：即遗民。
㊷比数：相比之中还算在数。
㊸稷(jì)下：战国时齐国的都城，在今山东临淄。
㊹挥汗成雨：《战国策·齐策》："临淄之途，车毂击，人肩摩，连衽成帷，举袂成幕，挥汗成雨，家敦而富，志高而扬。"形容繁盛、人众多之况。
㊺流人：流亡者。
㊻东山：鲁地山名。《孟子·尽心上》："孔子登东山而小鲁，登泰山而小天下。"一抔（póu）土：一捧土。

mountain and river,
With blood and to sprinkle it to a handful of
earth of their native land.

【其二】

想见皇华过二京①，
壶浆②夹道万人迎。
连昌宫③里桃应在，
华萼楼④前鹊定惊。
但说帝心怜赤子⑤，
须知天意念苍生⑥。
圣君大信明如日，
长乱何须在屡盟⑦。

【译注】

①皇华：赞颂使臣之语，亦指皇帝派出之使臣。《诗经·小雅·皇皇者华》："皇皇者华，君遣使臣也。送之以礼乐，言远而有光华也。"二京：南宋使臣赴金，要经过南京（今河南商丘）、东京（今河南开封）。

②壶浆：古时百姓以壶盛浆慰劳义师。《孟子·梁惠王上》："以万乘之国，伐万乘之国，箪食壶浆，以迎王师。"

③连昌宫：唐宫名，高宗时置，在洛阳。元稹《连昌宫词》："连昌宫内满宫竹，岁久无人森似束。又有墙头千叶桃，风动花落红蔌蔌。"

④华萼楼：即花萼相辉楼。

⑤赤子：百姓。

⑥苍生：百姓。《尚书·益稷》："光天之下，至于海隅苍生。"

⑦长乱何须在屡盟：意即国家长期动乱哪里是屡屡结盟能够解决的。《诗经·小雅·巧言》："君子屡盟，乱是用长。"

Two Poems Written to the Song Diplomat Han Xiaozhou

Two

I want to see the magnificent diplomats pass
Two Jing-Cities,
Being welcomed by the citizens to hand in
home foods and drinks.
The Lianchang Palace's peach blossoms
should be in bloom,
The Hua'e Pavilion's magpies would not be
in gloom.
It's said the emperor had sympathy to naive
children,
It's known the good-minded God would miss
the heaven.
Saint Monarch was truly believed to be as
bright as the sun,
Then long chaos originated from his
compromise decision.

题八咏楼

千古风流八咏楼[1]，
江山留与后人愁。
水通南国三千里，
气压江城十四州[2]。

A Poem Dedicated to the Octagon Watchtower

The distinguished watchtower set up 1000 years ago,
The rivers and mountains left late generations' sorrow.
Waters rolled through 3000 miles in south kingdom,
The airy style seemed to overwhelm 14-city realm.

【译注】

①风流：指情高远致。八咏楼：原名元畅楼，在今浙江金华，宋太宗至道年间更名八咏楼，与双溪楼、极目亭同为婺（wù）州观临胜地。

②十四州：指两浙路计辖二府十二州，即平江府、镇江府、杭州、越州、湖州、婺州、明州、常州、温州、台州、处州、衢州、严州、秀州，统称十四州（《宋史地理志》）。唐末五代著名画僧《献钱尚父》诗用过"十四州"等字样。

译者附注该诗作者及其原诗如下：

贯休：（832–912），俗姓姜，字德隐，唐末五代著名画僧。

贯休向钱镠所献诗如下：

《献钱尚父》

贵逼人来不自由，龙骧凤翥势难收。
满堂花醉三千客，一剑霜寒十四州。
鼓角揭天嘉气冷，风涛动地海山秋。
东南永作金天柱，谁羡当时万户侯。

端午帖子词①·皇帝阁

日月尧天②大，
璇玑舜历长③。
侧闻④行殿帐，
多集上书囊⑤。

【译注】

①端午帖子词：宋时每逢立春、端午，均命翰林作帖子词进献宫中，剪贴于禁中门帐，供皇帝及内宫欣赏，所作多为歌功颂德之辞。

②尧天：比喻太平盛世。尧传说是中国上古部落联盟首领。

③璇玑：舜帝时测天之器。舜：相传为中国历史上的先贤，是尧之后古帝王，古部落联盟首领，是禅让制的代表，以受尧的“禅让”而称王于天下，当时，国号为“虞”，故称“虞舜”。历长：舜帝的历数长。

舜历长：谓宋高宗在位时间像舜帝那么长。

④侧闻：间接听说。

⑤多集上书囊：古时大臣上书，用青布袋封之。此以汉文帝集书囊作宫殿帷帐的故事以颂高宗注重节俭。

Poetic Letter to Imperial Palace①

How to make the palace screen? I indrectly
know,
An emperor had book sacks to cover the
window.
Emperor Yao had been as great as the heaven
with the moon and the sun,
Xuan-star or Ji-star of Dipper foretold Shun
would be a son for a long reign.
How to make the palace screen? I indirecly
know,
An emperor had book sacks to shelter the
window.

【Annotation】

① In the Song Dynasty, imperial academicians were asked to something poetic to dedicate to exhibit in emperors' palace every spring or on the Dragon Boat Festival, which was an imperial traditional habit for the emperor to enjoy. Usually, more writings of praise were in poetic style as Li Qingzhao did in Shaoxing thirteen years to Imperial Palace or Queen's Pavilion or Concubines' Bed-palace. And someone said Li Qingzhao was to write on behalf of the other people, but not to be sure.

端午帖子词·皇后阁

意帖①初宜夏，
金驹已过蚕②。
至尊③千万寿，
行见百斯男④。

To Queen's Pavilion On Dragon Boat Festival

Satisfactory couplets posted in summer beginning,
The fast gold colts surpassed silkworms breeding.
The supreme monarch has his longevity immortal,
His hundreds of late successors remain perpetual.

【题解】

此诗作于宋高宗绍兴十三年（1143年），李清照在临安（杭州）时，系端午节前奉献给皇后的应酬之作。

【译注】

①意帖：即如意帖，古时民间常于端午节时在壁上张贴帖子，上书吉祥如意之语。

②金驹：即白驹，指日影，用喻时光。过蚕：过了养蚕的时节。

③至尊：皇帝。

④百斯男：谓多子（古有“文王百子”的说法）。

端午帖子词·夫人阁

三宫催解粽①，
妆罢天未明②。
便面天题字③，
歌头御赐名④。

An Impromptu Poem Post

Posting in Concubines' Bed-palace

In three palaces the Pyramid-shaped Zongzi ①
made ready,
The imperial beauties' makeup finished before
dawn early.
The emperor made his inscription on the
paper-fan,
Busily rewriting their singing songs' lyric title
again.

【译注】

①三宫：皇帝、太后、皇后合称三宫。解粽：京师人以端午日为解粽节。

②妆罢天未明：一作"团箭彩丝萦"。

③便面：扇子。天题字：天，指皇帝。天题字，即皇帝题字于扇。

④歌头：唐宋曲中篇名。指歌曲头一部分的第一段。御赐名：皇帝赐名。

[Annotation]

① Zongzi: a pyramid-shaped dumpling made of glutinous rice wrapped in bamboo or reed leaves. It's a traditional Chinese habit to make such a kind of food on the Dragon Boat Festival in order to commemorate great poet Qu Yuan (340 BC~278 BC).

偶成[1]

十五年前花月底，
相从曾赋赏花诗。
今看花月浑相似[2]，
安得[3]情怀似往时。

A Flash Idea Came in Mind

Under the moon with flowery shadow, fifteen
years ago,
We were to write and appreciate poems we
were to show.
Today the moon and flowers are as alike as
the lost day,
My mind full of affection differs from the old
poetry.

【译注】

①此诗当作于宋高宗建炎三年（1129年）赵明诚去世后，诗人抚今忆昔，表达了痛定思痛，对亡夫思恋哀悼之情。

②浑相似：完全相似。

③安得：怎得。

皇帝阁春帖子

莫进黄金簟[①]，
新除玉局床[②]。
春风送庭燎，
不复用沈香。

Spring Lyric to Post on Emperor Pavilion

Your Majesty did not make the gold-thread mat so gentle,
You made your dragon bed just like a simple rectangle.
Spring breeze blew the burning candle in the palace yard,
The bright monarch had no longer burnt the fragrant wood.

【译注】

①莫进：亦作“是进”或“其进”（源于《古今女史》《历朝名媛诗词》，详见《李清照集校注》）。黄金簟：指皇帝龙床。

②玉局床：指皇帝龙床。

贵妃阁春帖子

金环半后礼①，
钩弋比昭阳②。
春生百子帐③，
喜入万年觞④。

Spring Poem in Imperial Concubine Back-palace

Gold-ring measure meter was as a queen's precious gift,
Both Gouyi harem and Zhaoyang harem were elegant.
In spring babies were born in 100-baby-brand bed-curtain,
Happiness immersed into the 10000-year wine cups contain.

【译注】

①金环：后宫中皇后嫔妃所用的一种饰物，用以作产期或经期的标志。半后礼：享受皇后一半的待遇。后，皇后。

②钩弋：钩弋为汉武帝妃，亦称拳夫人，汉昭帝之母。钩弋夫人，西汉武垣县人。汉武帝东巡过武垣，被选入宫。因貌美聪敏，善于歌舞受宠，为其修"钩弋宫"，号"钩弋夫人"。钩弋夫人擅长纂拳藏阄游戏，又称"拳夫人"。后晋封为赵婕妤。钩弋，亦为汉代宫名。昭阳：汉代宫名。成帝宠妃赵飞燕所居之处，甚豪华。

③百子帐：古人举行婚礼时所用的一种锦绣篷帐，上绣百小儿嬉戏图，以祝多子多孙。

④万年觞：指向皇帝奉献的寿酒。觞，酒器。

乌江①

生当作人杰，
死亦为鬼雄。
至今思项羽，
不肯过江东。

Wujiang River

Alive, as a hero I live my life,
Dead, as a ghost king I died.
Still I miss of brave Xiang Yu①,
Not crossing the East-Riverside.

【译注】

①此诗因版本不同，题目又作《绝句》《夏日绝句》。

【Annotation】

① As a well-known ancient brave general, Xiang Yu (232BC ~ 202BC) killed himself when he was finally defeated near the Wujiang River.

分得知字[①]

学语[②]三十年，
缄口[③]不求知。
谁遣好奇士，
相逢说项斯[④]。

Mutually Writing One's Own Poem in the Same Rhyme

It spent thirty years on learning to write my poem,
Voicelessly doing so, I just seek for the rhyme.
If an poetic expert was dispatched to guide me,
We would talk about an ancient poet Xiang Si[①].

【译注】

①此词作年不详，从题目看，为李清照与诗友在一起分韵作诗时作。

②学语：《彤管遗编》等作"学诗"，此处指作诗。

③缄口：闭口不语。

④项斯：唐代江东人，字子迁，其初未成名之时，以诗卷谒杨敬之，杨爱其才，赠诗曰："几度见诗诗尽好，及观标格过于诗，平生不解藏人善，到处逢人说项斯。"项斯由此声名大振，擢拔上第。

【Annotation】

① Xiang Si: The Tang-Dynasty famous poet born in Jiangdong. He was praised and recommended by another great poet Yang Jingzhi. Since then, Xiang Si began to be well-known in China. Poet Yang loved Xiang's talent and wrote a poem to him like this:"Your poems, I read some, were all in charm, Compared with others, yours is the best poem. In Life if no understanding of good quality, I advise everyone to read your poetry." This Song-poem(Ci-poem) written by Li Qingzhao according to her pals rhyming scheme.

晓梦①

晓梦随疏钟②，飘然蹑云霞。
因缘安期生③，邂逅萼绿华④。
秋风正无赖，吹尽玉井花⑤。
共看藕如船，同食枣如瓜⑥。
翩翩坐上客，意妙语亦佳。
嘲辞斗诡辩，活火分新茶。
虽非助帝功，其乐莫可涯⑦。
人生能如此，何必归故家。
起来敛衣⑧坐，掩耳厌喧哗。
心知不可见，念念犹咨嗟⑨。

【译注】

①这是一首记梦游仙诗。诗写出了神仙境界中仙人们逍遥自在的生活，表现了诗人对无拘无束的自由生活的向往，同时也反映了诗人寻求精神解脱而不得的苦闷心情。全诗写得洒脱飘逸，想象丰富，富有浪漫色彩。有仙骨神韵，独具一格。

②疏钟：稀疏的钟声。

③安期生：秦时仙人。

④萼绿华：古代传说中的仙女。

⑤玉井花：古代传说中的莲花。韩愈诗《古意》："太华峰头玉井莲，开花十丈藕如船。"

⑥枣如瓜：《史记·封禅书》："李少君曰：'吾尝游海上，见安期生，安期生食巨枣，大如瓜。'"

⑦莫可涯：无涯，无穷尽。

⑧敛衣：敛掩衣襟，即整装以示肃敬。

⑨咨嗟：叹息。

Dreaming of Dawn

The morning bell rings intermittently,
The sounds float in rosy clouds freely.
Two predestined partners were timely in reunion,
By chance, such a lucky boy met a fairy maiden.
The autumn wind is of the rascal,
To blow flowers over the Jade Well.
Mutually to look at the boat-like lotus root,
They share eating the big melon-like date.
In elegant manners, the young man sat down,
While talking meaningfully in impressive tone.
His ridicule fought against the other's sophistry,
She dreamed of burning fire to cook the new tea.
Although her dream had no help to Emperor's need,
Still let him living an unlimitedly happy night indeed.
If the human life is just as her doing so,
Then unnecessary to think of home to go.
She got up to put on her gown,
To mask the ear noise long.
Her heart sensed her love was invisible,
No obsessing of her was impossible.

春残[1]

春残何事苦思乡，
病里梳头恨发长。
梁燕语多[2]终日在，
蔷薇风细一帘香。

Late Spring

In late spring, why you miss your hometown?
Being lovesick, I comb to hate my hair long.
Flying over the room beam to sing is the busy
swallow,
A breeze blows roses' fragrance to the curtain-
window.

【译注】

①此诗作年不详，从诗意看，当在李清照南渡之后，诗中表现了作者深切的思乡之情。

②梁燕语多：指栖于梁头上的燕子不停地呢喃。

感怀

宣和辛丑[①]八月十日到莱[②]，独坐一室，平生所见，皆不在目前。几上有《礼韵》[③]，因信手开之，约以所开为韵作诗，偶得"子"字，因以为韵，作《感怀》诗。

寒窗败几无书史，
公路[④]可怜合至此。
青州从事[⑤]孔方兄，
终日纷纷喜生事[⑥]。
作诗谢绝聊闭门，
燕寝[⑦]凝香有佳思。
静中吾乃得至交，
乌有先生子虚子[⑧]。

【题解】

此诗作于宋徽宗宣和三年（1121年）八月。李清照与丈夫赵明诚屏居青州十年后，赵出守莱州。李清照于莱州作此诗。诗的开头两句首先描绘了诗人所处的环境，寒窗败几、空无所有，从写生活环境中反映出诗人心境。然后转入议论，对酒与钱这类世人皆为之吸引的东西，表示了轻蔑。此诗虽为因闲而作，却绝非赋闲之篇，诗人的理想、情操、品格皆融于诗中，是一首较好的述怀诗。

My True Feelings in Mind

August (lunar month) 10, 1121, I stayed at Laizhou, sitting alone in a room to read everything quite different from today. On a small table, I freely opened a book on official rhyme. By chance I was asked to write a poem in "ZI" rhyme to express my mind.

The room had no books but poor table and window,
Historically greedy-reading scholars might be pitiful.
The wine drunkard just was greedy for money,
Eventually they try to make trouble day by day.
Shutting my door, I refused to reply pen pals in rhyme,
Yet my imperial partner wrote carefully some better poem.
In my peaceful life, I have got a true pal,
"Mr. Nothing" has still had everything virtual.

【译注】

①宣和辛丑：即宋徽宗宣和三年（1121年）。
②莱：莱州，今山东莱州市（原名掖县）。
③《礼韵》：宋代官颁韵书《礼部韵略》，共五卷。
④公路：一说是指三国时袁术，字公路。陈祖美则认为李清照“把《诗经·魏风·汾沮洳》中称呼贵族官吏的‘公路’，用来比拟与皇族同姓又身为知府的赵明诚的可能性更大些”。（《李清照评传》）
⑤青州从事：指好酒。
⑥生事：引起事端。
⑦燕寝：古代多指帝王寝息之所。此处指赵明诚莱州知事公馆。
⑧乌有先生子虚子：意为一无所有。子虚：不真实的事。乌有：没有。乌有、子虚指假设的、并不存在的事情或人。

钓台①

巨舰②只缘因利往，
扁舟③亦是为名来。
往来有愧先生④德，
特地通宵过钓台⑤。

Fishing Terrace

The giant ship is to seek for finance gain,
The flat boat is to win for glory reputation.
Wandering back and forth, I was shy a lot to learn from your morality,
Especially to visit your fishing spot for sensing your good quality.

【题解】

此诗另题作《夜发严滩》。宋高宗绍兴四年（1134年），李清照由临安去金华避乱，途经严子陵钓台，作此诗。诗中对汉隐士严子陵表示崇敬之情，对为名缰利索所羁的世人作了形象的刻画。诗人承认自己挣脱不开名缰利索，同时也是不愿为名缰利索所羁。

【译注】

①钓台：相传为汉严光（字子陵）垂钓之地，西汉末年，严光与刘秀是朋友，刘秀称帝后，请严光做官，被拒绝，隐居在浙江（桐庐）富春江，后人将其垂钓之所取名为钓台，亦名严滩。

②巨舰：大船。

③扁舟：小船。

④先生：指严光。宋范仲淹为桐庐守时，于钓台建“严先生祠堂”，并为之作记，其中云：“先生之德，山高水长。”

⑤通宵过钓台：严光不为名利所动，隐居不出，后人每每自愧不如，故过钓台者，常于夜间往来。

咏史

两汉本继绍①，
新室如赘疣②。
所以嵇中散③，
至死薄殷周④。

【译注】

①继绍：承传；继承。

②新室：西汉末年，王莽建立的新朝。赘疣（zhuì yóu）：皮肤上长的肉瘤。赘：多余。疣：肉瘤。比喻累赘无用之物。

③嵇中散：嵇康，字叔夜。三国曹魏时著名思想家、音乐家、文学家。为“竹林七贤”的精神领袖。嵇康娶曹操曾孙女，官为曹魏中散大夫，世称嵇中散。后因得罪钟会，为其诬陷，而被司马昭处死，年仅39岁。

④至死薄殷周：嵇康的朋友山涛向司马氏推举嵇康担任他的旧职。嵇康身为曹魏宗室，不齿山涛依附于司马氏的行为，于是遂与之绝交，并作《与山巨源绝交书》。其中有言：“非汤武而薄周孔。”薄：鄙薄，瞧不起。殷周：指殷汤王和周武王，二人分别建立了商朝和周朝。

Reviewing on the Two-Han Dynasty

The East Han dynasty inherited the West Han's history,
Wang Mang's New Regime like a wart was unnecessary.
As an ancient scholar Ji kang ① had sung a satirical song,
In the whole life he despised the Shang and Zhou dynasty.

[Annotation]

① Ji Kang (224 ~ 263): in the period of Three-Kingdoms, he was one of the famous thinkers, musicians, writers. As a spiritual leader of the so-called "Bamboos-Seven- Scholars", Ji Kang married Emperor Cao Cao's granddaughter and his official was in the fifth-class position. It was a pity that at his age of 39, he was killed by an higher official Sima Zhao.

上赵挺之

（一）

何况人间父子情。

【题解】

①公元1101年，李清照十八岁，嫁给了吏部侍郎赵挺之的儿子——太学生赵明诚。赵挺之与李格非在政治上属于不同党派，李清照与赵明诚结婚一年后，在激烈的党派斗争中，李格非被罢了官。李清照为了救父，给赵挺之写了一首诗，其中有一句是“何况人间父子情”（《逸句》）。可是“父子之情”并没有打动权欲熏心的赵挺之，李格非照例被罢免，而赵挺之却被独揽大权的蔡京看中，当上了右丞相，李清照又献诗讽喻赵挺之道：“炙手可热心可寒。”

②李清照《上赵挺之》选自《洛阳名园记·张琰序》、《癸巳类稿》卷十五、《绣水诗钞》卷一、《山东通志》卷一百四十一。《洛阳名园记·张琰序》云：“文叔在元祐，官太学。丁建中靖国，再用邪朋，串为党人。女适赵相挺之子，亦能诗，上赵相救其父云：‘何

Submit a Poetic Letter to Her Father-in-law Zhao Tingzhi①

Let alone the affectionate relation,
Between the father and the son.

【Annotation】

① At age of 18, in 1101, Li Qingzhao married Zhao Tingzhi's son, Zhao Mingcheng as a service member of the Ministry of Official Personnel Affairs in feudal China. However, her own father was not to belong to the same party. One year later from her marriage, a serious fighting between the two different parties happened; her father was dismissed from office. In order to save and help her own father, she wrote a poetic letter to submit to her father-in-law, the first sentence of her letter was: “Let alone the affectionate relation between the father and the son.” Her father-in-law's mind was full of political power, still dismissed her own father from office. And then he was appointed as Prime Minister of the Song Dynasty. Hence, Li Qingzhao wrote another poem to satirize him, one line of which was as follows:

“Being roasted, hands could be hotter,
Yet one's heart might still be colder.”

况人间父子情。'识者哀之。"按定党籍事在崇宁元年(1102年),《上赵挺之》殆作于是时,其时赵挺之虽为执政(尚书左丞),尚未为相。张琰称为赵相,乃追叙之语。又按黄庭坚诗中亦有此句(《忆邢敦父》诗:"眼看白璧埋黄壤,何况人间父子情。"),见《豫章黄先生文集》卷九。山谷于清照为前辈,疑清照或用其成句,否则即暗合也。

上赵挺之
（二）

炙手可热心可寒。

Submit a Poetic Letter to Her Father-in-law Zhao Tingzhi①

Being roasted, hands could be hotter,
Yet one's heart might be colder.

【题解】

李清照生父李格非被罢免后不久，赵挺之当上了右丞相，李清照又献诗讽喻赵挺之道："炙手可热心可寒。"

【Annotation】

①Poetess Li Qingzhao's father, Li Gefei was dismissed from office, and then her father-in-law Zhao Tingzhi was appointed as Prime Minister of the Song Dynasty, China. She wrote this poem to submit to him again.

失题（一）

诗情如夜鹊，
三绕未能安。

The Title Lost

Poetic emotion is like night magpie,
Uneasily flying around in the sky.

【题解】

李清照的《失题》选自《风月堂诗话》卷上、《宋诗纪事》卷八十七、《癸巳类稿》卷十五、《绣水诗钞》卷一。

失题

（二）

少陵也自可怜人[1]，
更待来年试春草[2]。

The Title Lost

With a strong will, Shao-ling was a pitiful
man,
Still to wish next spring early to return again.

【题解】

此二断句当作于北宋时期，参阅《李清照事迹编年》公元1140年事迹。

【译注】

①少陵：指杜甫（712～770），字子美，自号少陵野老，是我国唐代伟大的现实主义诗人，世界文化名人，与李白并称“李杜”。自：《癸巳类稿》作“是”。

②来：《风月堂诗话》以外各本俱作“明”。试：试图。

失题

（三）

南渡衣冠少王导①，
北来消息欠刘琨②。

【译注】

①王导：东晋时期著名政治家、书法家，历仕晋元帝、明帝和成帝三朝，是东晋政权的奠基人之一。

②刘琨：西晋将领、音乐家、文学家。刘琨有音乐癖，有“一曲胡笳救孤城”的典故，他留传下来的诗词有5首，临死前的名句“何意百炼刚，化为绕指柔”流传千古。

The Title Lost

The South Song Dynasty lacked of Wang Dao ① such a true man,
The North land news showed we needed a heroic poet Liu Kun ②.

【Annotation】

① Wang Dao(276 ~ 339): one of the Eastern Jin Dynasty's famous politicians, calligraphers; one of the founders of the Eastern Jin regime.

② Liu Kun (271~ 318): The Western Jin's general, musician, writer. Liu Kun had a music addiction.

失题

（四）

南来尚怯吴江冷①，
北狩应悲易水寒②。

The Title Lost

Crossing the southern China, still I sensed
cold Wujiang River,
Being lost the North land, also I felt ice-frozen
Yishui-water.

【译注】

①来：元代《鸡肋编》作“游”，从其他各本。尚：清代《癸巳类稿》作“犹”。怯：元代《鸡肋编》作“觉”，从其他各本。吴江：即松江，为太湖最大的支流。

②北狩：到北方狩猎，借指向北进军；皇帝被掳到北方去的婉词。（详见《癸巳类稿》，道光十三年出版，作者（清）俞正燮。）悲：清代《癸巳类稿》作“知”。

失题
（五）

露花倒影柳三变①，
桂子飘香张九成②。

【题解】

冠以《失调名》或《失题》标题的李清照残缺的诗词多散落在后人的一些著作中，或因为作者直接引用或几经转抄使其得以保存下来。此类《失题》多出自《老学庵笔记》卷二、《词苑丛谈》卷三、《癸巳类稿》卷十五、《绣水诗钞》卷一等经典著作中。

【译注】

①柳三变，即柳永，崇安（今福建武夷山）人。原名三变，字景庄。后改名永，字耆卿。排行第七，又称柳七。宋仁宗朝进士，官至屯田员外郎，故世称柳屯田。他自称“奉旨填词柳三变”，以毕生精力作词，并以“白衣卿相”自许。北宋词人婉约派最具代表性的人物之一，代表作《雨霖铃》。

②张九成：字子韶，其先开封人，徙居钱塘。游京师，从师杨时。宋孝宗赵昚（shèn）绍兴二年（1132 年），廷试第一，授镇东军签判。累官宗正少卿，权礼部侍郎。因与秦桧不和，谪居安南军。在安南十四年。桧死，起知温州。后丐祠归，数月而卒。著有《横浦集》二十卷，《四库总目》及《孟子传》，并传于世。

The Title Lost

Three-Change Willow looks like an inverted
shadow of the morning dew,
Nine-Success Zhang like osmanthus fragrance
floated from the window.

失题

（六）

犹将歌扇[1]向人遮。

The Title Lost

It's still like a beautiful dancing girl,
Swinging a fan to cover her show.

【译注】

①歌扇：歌者歌舞时用的扇子。庾信《春赋》："月入歌扇，花承节鼓。"李邕《奉和初春幸太平公主南庄应制》诗："流风入座飘歌扇，瀑水侵阶溅舞衣。"也指歌女写上曲目供人点唱的折扇。

失题
（七）

水晶山枕象牙床。

The Title Lost

It’s a pair of crystal U-shaped pillow,
On an ivory bed like a jewelry show.

失题（八）

彩云易散月长亏。

The Title Lost

Colorful clouds scatter, the sky easily hollow,
The crescent moon looks like a long bow.

失题
（九）

几多深恨断人肠。

The Title Lost

Much hatred were to deepen,
One would be heartbroken.

失题
（十）

罗衣消尽恁时香。

The Title Lost

Gradually, as time goes on,
Her gown's fragrance gone.

失题
（十一）

闲愁也似月明多。

The Title Lost

In leisure sorrow, I am alone,
As much lonely as the bright moon.

失题
（十二）

直送凄凉到画屏。

The Title Lost

My gloomy and forlorn emotion,
Directly was sent to the painted screen.

失题（十三）

行人舞袖拂梨花。

The Title Lost

Pear flowers falling on pedestrians' sleeves,
In order to sweep off white petals, they dance.

附　录

《李清照生平剪影》（摘编）

李清照生于北宋元丰[1]七年，逝于临安，享年72岁（1084年生，1155年卒）。号易安居士，山东济南人，南宋杰出女文学家，婉约[2]词派的宗主。历史上与济南历城豪放派词人辛弃疾[3]并称“济南二安”。其父李格非（齐州历城县人），是北宋著名的学者和散文家。李清照幼承家学，早有才名。以词著名，兼工诗文，并著有《词论》，在中国文学史上享有崇高声誉，“文有李清照，武有秦良玉[4]。”早年生活安定、优裕，词作多写相思之情；金兵入侵后，遭遇国家巨变，词作多感慨身世飘零。她的诗文感时咏史，与词风迥异。她还擅长书画，兼通音律。现存诗文及词为后人所辑，有《漱玉[5]词》等。主张“词，当别具一家也”。她是中国历史上唯一一位名字被用来命名外太空环形山的女性。

“大河百代，众浪齐奔，淘尽万古英雄汉；

词苑千载，群芳竞秀，盛开一枝女儿花。”

此对联形容的便是李清照。

她的《乌江》里的两句“生当作人杰，死亦为鬼雄”已成为千古流传的经典名句；她《声声慢》中的那句“寻寻觅觅，冷冷清清，凄凄惨惨戚戚”，成了她个人的专有品牌，彪炳[6]于文学史，空前绝后，没有任何人敢于企及。于是，她便被当作了愁的化身。当我们穿过历史的尘烟咀嚼她的愁情时，才发现在中国三千年的古代文学史中，特立独行，登峰造极的女性也就只有她一人。

李清照出生于书香门第，与太学生赵明诚[7]结婚后一同研究金石书画，过着幸福美好的生活。1127年，靖康之变[8]后，她与赵明诚避乱江南，丧失了珍藏的大部分文物。后来赵明诚病死，她独自漂流在杭州、越州、金华一带，在凄苦孤寂中度过了晚年。她《声声慢》一词就创作在此时。她是一位在诗、词、文、赋上都有成就的作家，但最擅长、最有名的是词。她早年曾做《词论》，主张“词，当别具一家也”，注重词体协音律、重铺叙、有情致，性格开朗，敢于直言，曾坦诚地批评了从苏轼到秦观、黄庭坚等词家的不足。

她是最有才华的女人，幼时过目不忘，出语惊人，博览群书。齐鲁壮丽的山川涵育了她的创作灵性，少女时代就已名噪一时，崭露峥嵘。

婚后与丈夫情投意合，如胶似漆，“夫妇擅朋友之胜[9]”。然而好景不长，朝中新旧党争愈演愈烈，一对鸳鸯被活活拆散，赵李隔河相望，饱尝相思之苦。

后来金人铁蹄南下，南宋王朝腐败无能，自毁长城。赵明诚空怀满腔热血，可惜出师未捷身先死。目睹国破家亡，但李清照“虽处忧患穷困而志不屈”，在“寻寻觅觅、冷冷清清”的晚年，她殚精竭虑，编撰《金石录》，完成丈夫未竟之功。

因此，可以说李清照的作品是和愁字分不开的，从开始的情愁，到家破人亡的家愁，再到江山沦陷的国愁。这纷繁的愁绪令她一步步地迈上了文学的圣殿。真可谓万古愁心！

李清照文词绝妙，鬼斧神工，前无古人，后无来者，被尊为婉约宗主，是中华精神文明史上的一座丰碑。

李清照有“千古第一才女”之称。她善用白描手法写诗词，自辟蹊径，语言清丽。论词强调协律，崇尚典雅，反对以作诗文之法作词。也能诗，但留存不多，部分篇章感时咏史，情辞慷慨，与其词风不同。

李清照有《易安居士文集》《易安词》等著作，但久已不传。现存诗文集为后人所辑《李清照集校注》，有《漱玉词》1卷，《漱玉集》5卷。代表作有《声声慢》《一剪梅》《如梦令》《醉花阴》《武陵春》《乌江》等。

【译注】

①元丰：宋神宗皇帝赵顼的年号。

②婉约：即婉转含蓄。“婉约”一词，早见于先秦古籍《国语·吴语》的“故婉约其辞”，“婉”为柔美、婉曲；“约”的本意是为缠束，引申为精炼、隐约、微妙。故“婉约”与“烦滥”相对立。

婉约派，宋词的一大流派。明确提出词分婉约、豪放者，一般认为是明人张綖。其内容主要写男女情爱，离情别绪，伤春悲秋，光景流连；其形式大都婉丽柔美，含蓄蕴藉，情景交融，声调和谐。词本为合乐而歌，娱宾遣兴，内容不外离愁别绪，闺情绮怨。结构深细缜密，音律婉转和谐，语言圆润清丽，有一种柔婉之美。如秦少游（秦观）之作多是婉约，苏子瞻（苏轼）之作多是豪放。大抵词体以婉约为正。李煜词则为香软词风。故明人以婉约派来概括这一类型的词风，人们形成了以婉约为正的观念。婉约词风长期支配词坛。

③辛弃疾（1140年—1207年），字幼安，号稼轩，山东济南府历城县人，南宋豪放派词人，人称词中之龙，与苏轼合称“苏辛”，与李清照并称“济南二安”。现存词600多首，富于强烈的爱国主义思想和战斗精神，热情洋溢，慷慨悲壮，笔力雄厚。著名词作有《水调歌头·带湖吾甚爱》《摸鱼儿·更能消几番风雨》《满江红·家住江南》《沁园春·杯汝来前》《西江月·夜行黄沙道中》等。

④武有秦良玉：我国历史上第一位见诸正史将相列传记述的女将军。

⑤漱玉：由济南李清照故居前的漱玉泉得名，是为济南七十二名泉之一，泉水清澈见底，泉水自池底涌出，溢出池外，跌落石上，水石相激，淙淙有声，犹如漱玉。相传李清照早年曾在泉边洗漱。该泉至今仍在流淌，现在济南趵突泉公园内的李清照纪念堂门口。

⑥彪炳：[书面语]文彩焕发；照耀。

⑦赵明诚：字德甫。山东诸城人，南宋丞相赵挺之子。著有《金石录》一书，南宋洪迈有《容斋随笔·赵德甫金石录》可参考。

⑧靖康之变：靖康二年（1127年）四月金军攻破开封，在开封城内大肆劫掠，掠走徽宗、钦宗和后妃、太子、宗戚、工臣、歌女等3000人以及城中的全部财物，开封以及附近的州县惨遭浩劫，北宋灭亡。因此事件发生在靖康二年，史称“靖康之变”或“靖康之难”。

⑨夫妇擅朋友之胜：明代江之淮在《古今女史》卷一中有云："自古夫妇擅朋友之胜，从来未有如李易安与赵德甫者，佳人才子，千古绝唱。"意为夫妇二人如胶似漆，比朋友还要亲密。

【Appendix】
Li Qingzhao's Life Silhouette

Li Qingzhao was born in the seventh year of Yuanfeng–reign period, the Northern Song Dynasty, and died at age of 72 in Lin'an city (born in 1084, died in 1155). Yi-an was her literary first name. Her birth-place was Jinan city, Shangdong Province, China. She was an outstanding female writer in graceful style. At that time in China, she was as famous as another great Song-poetry writer Xin Qiji. Her father, Li Gefei (born in Qizhou city) was a famous scholar and essayist of the Northern Song Dynasty. Young Li Qingzhao had a good family education, so she was long known and well known for works of poetry, and once wrote an academic paper on the Song-poetry. In the history of Chinese literature, she had a high reputation. As a saying goes, "Literary talent is Li Qingzhao and military talent is Qin Liangyu". Her early life was happy, stable, and she wrote more graceful Ci lyrics. After the invasion of the Jin enemy, her own motherland suffered from a national change, so her Ci lyrics were full of more feelings of life wandering. Her poetic sense was of national history. Her Ci lyrics were quite different from general poetry. She was also good at painting and calligraphy. Her existing poems and Ci lyrics were collected into a book entitled *Clear-scouring jade* and so on. She advocated "the Song-poetry should be more unique than the other poetry". It's an only lady's name in Chinese history that was used for outer space crater.

"Great rivers' 100-generation galloping surges clean all ancient heroic men;

Poetic gardens' 1000-year rival flowers envy only one charming maiden."

That's the description to lyric writer Li Qingzhao.

In her poem entitled *Wujiang River*, the initials two lines are

"Alive, as a hero I live my life,

Dead, as a ghost king I died."

The two poetic lines have become and will be everlasting from generation to generation as an eternal classic famous saying. A few initial lines of her another well known Song-poem

Sounds Go Slow are translated by Manfield Zhu like this :

I am to seek, seek and look for what I think,
I feel cold, lonely, so sad and so tragic.
To be sorrowful, unhappy and lovesick.
It's getting abruptly warm, still cold,
Keeping fit for me is difficult.

That already became her own exclusive brand, shining in the history of literature, unprecedented; no one dares to match with her lofty. So she was regarded as the incarnation of the worry. Through the history of dust to chew her melancholy, we could find she was the only maverick with the culmination achievement among all the women in the three-thousand–year long history of ancient Chinese literature.

Li Qingzhao was born in the scholarly family and she got married with a royal student Zhao Mingcheng to make research on stone-carving painting and calligraphy. Both of them were living a happy life. However, in 1127, Jingkang Coup happened to the Northern Song Dynasty (Jingkang as the Song Emperor Zhao Huan's reign-year name). Li Qingzhao and Zhao Mingcheng had to avoid Jingkang change; they lost most of the collections of cultural relics. Later, Zhao Mingcheng died. She drifted alone in Hangzhou, Yuezhou, Jinhua and more other cities in the southern China. She was miserable, lonely, spending her time in later years. Her Song-poem *Sounds Go Slow* was a vivid creation of her inner world's worry or sorrow at that time. She was not only good at writing poetry or Song-poetry, but also good at writing other works. Her strong point was to write the Song-poetry, and she had to make research on *The Song-Poetry*. She advocated "the Song-poetry should be more unique than the other poetry". She emphasized to pay more attention to the tonality, the narrative and the affection of poetry. As for her character, she was cheerful, and dare to speak frankly, frankly to criticize from great poet Su Shi to graceful-style poet Qin Guan as well as poet Huang Tingjian and so on, seriously pointing out their common writing shortcomings.

She was the most talented woman, during her childhood, she could recite what she just read, could say something to be surprised. She read more and more books on the past and on the present. Her Qilu native land's magnificent rivers and mountains nourished her to make her creative spirituality reach the culmination. In girlhood, she was well known for her intelligence with her revealing lofty.

After their marriage, Li Qingzhao and Zhao Mingcheng mutually loved as glue like paint, "their affection are much better than all the friends in great extent". However, their happy period did not last long, in the imperial court, the old and the new party struggled to be intensified, then, the young couple like a pair of mandarin ducks were living a lonely life, both Zhao and Li were apart by an invisible wide river, suffering from much bitterness.

Later, the Jin invaders were as if wearing iron shoes to tread on the south part of China seriously. Then the Southern Song Dynasty was of corruption incompetence, and self-destructed the Great Wall. Zhao Mingcheng's mind was filled with blood boiling, but unfortunately he died before fighting against the Jin enemy. Witnessed her country broken, her husband's death, Li Qingzhao still did not fear the worry and poverty, but to be indomitable. During later years, she wrote, "I am to seek, seek and look for what I think/ I feel cold, lonely, so sad and so tragic/ To be sorrowful, unhappy and lovesick/ It's getting abruptly warm still cold / Keeping fit for me is difficult." But still she tried her best to compile *Jade-carving with calligraphy recorded*, eventually completing her husband's unfinished works.

Therefore, it could be said that Li Qingzhao's works were inseparable from affectionate worry, from family melancholy, and from her national depression. This sadness made her step on the holy temple of literature. That could be described as her eternal sadness, worry or sorrow!

Li Qingzhao was considered as "the first talented lady during the 1000-year long history". She was good at using purely white-sketch way to write poems, good at seeking for her own way while using her graceful language. She emphasized to abide by the rhyme rule, advocating elegance, against following after the traditional poetic way to write the Song-poetry or the Ci lyrics. Also she was good at writing general metrical poems with rhymes, but not much retention, some of which were about Chinese history, not in the same style with her

Ci lyrics or Song-poetry.

Li Qingzhao had *Hermit Yi-an's collected works, Yi-an's Song-poetry*, but for a long time it had not passed on to readers. The existing poetry collection was entitled *Li Qingzhao's complete works with annotations checked up, Clear-scouring jade* (Volume I), *Jade-scouring collected works* (Volume I ~ V) . Li Qingzhao's representative works are often mentioned like this: *Sounds Go Slow, A Blooming Plum, Like a Dream Verse, Being Intoxicated in Flowery Shade*, *Fairyland Spring* and *Wujiang River*, etc..

后 记

译者附言

2008年8月《中国翻译》编辑部曾给我一次机会参加第十八届世界翻译大会，从此，我进一步增强了让“中国文化走向世界——影响人类未来”的使命感，开始系统地英译中国诗词。商务印书馆国际有限公司已经出版了我的《中国历代诗词英译集锦》《李煜诗词英译全集》，中国外文出版发行事业局北京朝华出版社出版了我英译的《赵朴初咏茶诗集》。这几本译作初版后不久就又再版，受到了国内外读者欢迎。

译诗对译者自己来说，几乎总是一件苦乐参半、充满遗憾的事情。有时即使几译其稿，也未必译出自己得意之作。当一本译作刚刚出版时，高兴了一阵子，但过了几年之后就会有更多的不满意，甚至想完全重译。这种真实的隐痛几乎一生都会让自己心灵不得安宁。当然，也有译得顺手的时候，一气呵成，几年之后也不想再改动一个字。

10年出了3本译作，又一版再版，非常感谢商务印书馆国际有限公司以及中国外文出版发行事业局北京朝华出版社成就了我的一生的夙愿，让我有机会开始译介中国传统文化并使其走向更广阔的世界。

译者要特别知道自己的弱点和短板，永远居安思危，不断提高自己，要有不断推陈出新的意识和责任感。

现借《李清照诗词英译全集》出版的机会，出示几首自己近10年来英译的诗词，诚请同行朋友们不吝赐教。非常希望能听到不同的声音。人无完人，金无足赤，译者水平有限，译文更不敢自信完美无缺。希望自己的译作有勇气越过翰林院的高墙去经风雨、见世面。

本文引用了几首自译的诗词，译者直接或间接获得了读者们对这些诗词的点评，非常珍惜、录以备忘。

A Farewell Poem to the Old Meadow
Bai Juyi (772~846)
离离原上草，一岁一枯荣。
野火烧不尽，春风吹又生。
远芳侵古道，晴翠接荒城。
又送王孙去，萋萋满别情。

Grass is spreading over the meadow,
Life or death will yearly come, yearly go.
The bale-fire can burn away the green,
Spring breeze will help it survive again.
The sweet green afar intrudes the old way,
The waste town meets it on a sunny day.
Seeing off my bosom friend again,
Still I feel strongly reluctant in pain.

汉诗与英诗的格律不尽相同，但仍有可类比之处。通常,英诗相邻的四行，行与行之间的押韵格式（rhyming scheme)有四种：（1）相邻两行押韵(AABB)，（2）隔行押韵(ABCB)，（3）隔行交互押韵(ABAB)，（4）交错押韵(ABBA)等。

译者英译白居易《赋得古原草送别》用了“AABB”韵式。白居易《长恨歌》中文的韵式也多为相邻两行押韵。此英译的音步、抑扬格位、尾韵大体符合英诗的规范。译者尽量避免用以辅音收尾的单词作为尾韵，力求读起来音响效果好一些。（但汉语鼻音韵母的韵尾可用辅音字母，如n,ng。）如，英译《赋得古原草送别》最后两行的收尾字分别是again和 pain，读起来较上口，音响效果也不错。

英译《赋得古原草送别》曾受到“无忧考网”的青睐，将其贴在“首页·英语翻译资格考试·导航·备考辅导”栏目（2008-09-24 10:50 无忧考网）。

汉语韵母按结构可分为单韵母、复韵母、鼻韵母，普通话中共有39个韵母。韵母由韵头、韵腹、韵尾组成。 韵尾的读音通常都是读元音或母音，只有鼻韵母的韵尾读音相当于英语的辅音字母（如鼻音字母n,ng）。汉语音韵的这一特点为译者处理汉诗英译扩大了选择的余地。因为英文辅音字母收尾的单词比比皆是，远远超过其元音字母（a, e, i, o, u）。为此，译者可以根据译文所涵盖的单词比较容易找到合适的尾韵用字。

白居易《长恨歌》长诗原文通篇几乎都是相邻两行押韵——AABB或ABBA韵式，偶有ABAB或ABCB韵式。据此，译文可力求同原文尾韵韵式相似，可以缩小两种语言之间在格律上的反差。《长恨歌》一共120行，这里仅选几行英译，供对英译格律感兴趣的朋友们参考。

《长恨歌》
白居易 (772~846)
天生丽质难自弃，一朝选在君王侧。
回眸一笑百媚生，六宫粉黛无颜色。

韵式(AABB)
Her natural beauty could hardly keep her inside,
Once she was selected to the lust monarch’s side.
Glancing back with a smile of 100-times charming,
She let six-palace imperial beauties no good-looking.

云鬓花颜金步摇，芙蓉帐暖度春宵。
春宵苦短日高起，从此君王不早朝。

韵式（AABB）
Her phoenix coronet with a hairpin Gold Pendant,
She spent spring night to shelter in warm lotus tent.
Spring night was too short to stop daybreak,
The Emperor could not go for timely work.

揽衣推枕起徘徊，珠箔银屏迤逦开。
云鬓半偏新睡觉，花冠不整下堂来。

韵式（ABAB）
Getting up to put on her gown to push pillow aside,
She rolled up to have bead-curtain screen open.
Just awoken, her temples hairs inclined to one side,
She left from her bedroom with her coronet bun.

英译汉诗如何具体实现“音美”？不同译者有不同思路。如果有可能让英译的尾韵含有相当于汉语前响复韵母（ai、ao、ei、ou）发音的英文单词（如fly, die, why, cow, law, way, stay, go, low, and so on），那么，音响效果较好。

《相见欢》
李煜（937~978）
无言独上西楼，月如钩，
寂寞梧桐深院锁清秋。

剪不断，理还乱，是离愁。

别是一番滋味在心头。

Joyful Reunion

Li Yu (937~978)

Upstairs, voicelessly I'd like to go,
The moon is like a bow,
The deep courtyard can hold,
Lonely parasol tree to lock autumn cold.
It is impossible to cut off my sorrow,
I comb it up but fail,
No way to cancel my parting sorrow,
In my heart it's a tasteful farewell.

《采桑子》

辛弃疾（1140~1207）

少年不识愁滋味，爱上层楼。
爱上层楼，为赋新词强说愁。
而今识尽愁滋味，欲说还休。
欲说还休，却道天凉好个秋。

Picking Mulberry

Xin Qiji (1140~1207)

As a young fellow,
I did not know the taste of sorrow,
I'd like to go,
To the high watchtower from the low.
I'd like to go,

To the high watchtower from the low.
I was on purpose to say "sorrow",
For writing a new poem.
Now I know how about the sorrow,
But I don't want to say what I know.
Now I know how about the sorrow,
But I don't want to say what I know,
I just talk something about the autumn cold.

选择什么样的尾韵只能因势利导，根据原文词语所提供的可能，但译者仍可通过调整语序、变换同义词、充分利用形态语言的形等手段有意识地去寻找更理想的音韵。

辛弃疾这首《采桑子》词的英译出版后出乎预料，很有市场，中国传媒大学比较文学专业研究生上课时曾播放过朗诵的录音，颇受学生青睐。有的小学英语老师也在英语课堂上给学生朗读过英译的词句。

自己译作能够派上用场，这的确值得一提。

编辑出版了几本译作之后，经历了译事的酸甜苦辣，不敢说自己哪首译得最好，却忘不了那些费心思最多、读者也最熟悉的诗词。英译李清照《声声慢》时，总觉得想译出恰当的、贴切的译文很难，很难一次完成。看了十年前《声声慢》的英译文之后仍然会产生新的英译思路，因为译者自己也有个进步的过程，同时也由于对原文的理解上有更新，比如，开始认为词里边“晚来风急”等字样无可非议，但后来读到我国红学家俞平伯另有“晓来风急”之说，便想修改原译。

李清照《声声慢》以“寻寻觅觅”等14个叠字开头的千古名句，千百年不知受到多少文人墨客的青睐。近代人们对探讨如何英译这类叠字的兴致有增无减，思路多多，各有千秋。有人强调“以叠字译叠字”，有人主张效仿英诗头韵（initial rhyme）韵式，不一而足。本文对“以叠字译叠字”并不想乐此不疲。因为以中文为母语的译者，往往不自觉地忽略了叠字结构的用法并非英语的强项，国人往往以汉语思维自我欣赏，但真正以英语为母语的读者不以为然。西人熟悉long long ago/very very good；但对day day up之类的结构用语，只能一笑了之。国人谁也不会把“日日夜夜”英译成day day night night，谁也不会在“days and nights”这类小河沟里翻了船！英译汉诗词中的叠字时，既要考虑形式上的重叠又不可不受语法结构的制约。

现将本书中译者对“寻寻觅觅，冷冷清清，凄凄惨惨戚戚”的英译出示如下：

I am to seek, seek and look for what I think,
I feel cold, lonely, so sad and so tragic,
To be sorrowful, unhappy and lovesick.

通常，除了祈使句或口语或在特定的语境下，地道的英语其主语或事物的施主是不缺位的。英译时往往需要补充其逻辑主语。

总之，如果译者自己英语语感不足以给自己用叠字的勇气，就别勉强用中文式的叠字。

英美等英语国家（native speakers）倒喜欢用英文的头韵修辞法（in alliterative fashion）。如，在美国的大街上经常可以看到提醒司机的英语告示“You drink, you drive, you die”，一连用三个辅音字母d开头与后边的元音相拼成的单词（动词、名词或形容词等），音韵效果的确不错。

文人墨客对头韵的修辞法也颇有好感，两个或两个以上的头韵词串，读起来上口，听起来悦耳。

我们英译汉诗也不妨试用这类头韵的手法（in alliterative fashion）。例如，可以用“lovely posture and light manner”来英译杜牧《赠别》诗中的“娉娉袅袅”：

娉娉袅袅十三余，豆蔻梢头二月初。
春风十里扬州路，卷上珠帘总不如。

She is 13 years old in lovely posture and light manner,

She looks like February young cardamom top flower.

Spring breeze blows 10-Li Yangzhou's street maiden,

No one could match her beauty within pearl curtain.

回文诗词的出现与中国语言语序机动灵活的特点密不可分，也因为中文是非形态语言，完全没有繁琐的格位变化，文字本身没有词形或词尾的变化，因此其机动灵活的语序，就给回文诗词的创造打开了方便之门。中文语序的科学性、灵活性是回文诗词天然的生长温床。

下边出示本文作者英译的两首回文诗，用10个字写成28个字的七言律诗：

回文诗《春》

吴绛雪（1650~1674）

莺啼岸柳弄春晴，

柳弄春晴晓月明。

明月晓晴春弄柳，

晴春弄柳岸啼莺。

Spring

Wu Jiangxue（1650—1674）

(Palindromic Poem)

Crowing warblers in willow, help spring glow,

To help spring glow, at dawn, the moon bright.

Bright moon at dawn, glow spring helps willow,

Glow spring helps the willow warbler crow.

将“莺啼岸柳弄春晴晓月明”10个字，按回文诗一种结构式，即给定的语序就能读出这首回文诗《春》：

1 2 3 4 5 6 7~

4 5 6 7 8 9 10~

10 9 8 7 6 5 4~

7 6 5 4 3 2 1>

回文诗《半色秋》

唐寅（1470—1523）

悠云白雁过南楼，

雁过南楼半色秋。

秋色半楼南过雁，

楼南过雁白云悠。

Colored Autumn

Tang Yin（1470~1523）

(Palindromic Poem)

Leisurely clouds, white geese fly south pavilion,

White geese fly south pavilion in half autumn.

Autumn half in pavilion south, fly white geese,

Pavilion south fly geese in white leisurely clouds.

唐寅不仅写回文诗，也很会写藏头诗。这位明代江南大才子的《我爱秋香》出手不凡，写得非常自然流畅，毫无娇揉造作和斧凿之痕。

藏头诗《我爱秋香》

唐寅（1470~1523）

我画蓝江水悠悠，

爱晚亭上枫叶愁。

秋月溶溶照佛寺，
香烟袅袅绕经楼。

I Love Autumn Fragrant
Tang Yin（1470~1523）
(acrostic)
I painted the blue river slowly and slowly to flow,
Love-Evening-Kiosk is to hold maples' sorrow.
Autumn moonlight is hovering Buddha temple,
Fragrant incense-smoke's curling up Sutra hall.

这首英译藏头诗曾得到翻译家江枫先生的首肯，认为体现了他的“形神兼备”的译论。

唐代陈子昂（661~702）《登幽州台歌》一诗，两行五言，两行六言，不伦不类，不受平仄约束，也不讲究韵式，可陈子昂这首无规无矩的诗却倍受青睐。千百年来，它让人心胸开阔、感慨万千，人们不得不为它的雄浑、伟大的气势折服。可见，不论写诗或译诗，内容信息与其表达形式相比，内容是更不可有任何闪失的。陈子昂《登幽州台歌》这首诗未必符合诗家规范的格律，但脍炙人口、百读不厌。

《登幽州台歌》
陈子昂（661~702）
前不见古人，
后不见来者。
念天地之悠悠，
独怆然而涕下！

Stepping upon Youzhou-Watchtower

Chen Zi'ang (661~702)

Looking ahead, I could find no ancient man,

Glancing back, no one coming forth was seen.

I pondered my motherland so wide, so open,

My tears burst out as I watched the heaven.

以上提到的自己英译过的都是古典诗词，主要是围绕所谓音美、形美谈了很肤浅的看法，觉得如何实现意美译界分歧较少，共识较多，对“信达雅”的信，对“忠实原文”的忠，普遍认同。但这“信”或“忠”若细化也颇费口舌。文如其人，几乎没有哪首诗词的译文不在向读者解释译者围绕意美或神似都做了些什么。

鲁迅先生《自文字至文章》有一段三美的论断：“意美以感心，一也；音美以感耳，二也；形美以感目，三也。”鲁迅“三美”的论断，也许对翻译界构建文学翻译理论有一定的先瞻性。

下边想就一首时下流行的短句诗的汉译，谈及一点诗歌翻译中的风格问题。

I love three things in this world,

The sun, the moon and you.

The sun for the day,

The moon for the night,

And you forever.

这充满诗情画意的对白可能是从英国诗人威廉·迈克尔·罗塞蒂(William Michael Rossetti)(1829~1919)1887年写的《约翰·济慈的生活》（*Life of John Keats*）一诗中转录过来的。请看：

For the world you may just be somebody,

But for somebody you maybe the world.

I love three things, the sun the moon and you.

The sun for the day,

The moon for the night,

And you forever.

以下的译文未包括含前两行:

浮世三千，吾爱有三，

日，月与卿;

日为朝，月为暮，

卿为朝朝暮暮。

(网上的一种新译文，译者不详)

从作品问世的时间来判定，显然，是英国诗人威廉·迈克尔·罗赛蒂（William Michael Rossetti）（1829~1919）创作的《约翰·济慈的生活》（*Life of John Keats*）在先。美国女作家斯蒂芬妮·梅尔（Stephanie Meyer）（1973~）在《暮光之城》中的引用在后。

原来，《约翰·济慈的生活》也有其旧译文:

对于世界而言，你也许只是某个人，

但对某个人而言，你或许就是整个世界。

我热爱三个事物，太阳，月亮，和你。

太阳给我白昼，月亮给我夜晚，

而你，给我永远。

（佚名 译）

相比之下，这篇旧汉译朴实无华、自然流畅，没有特意夸大或缩小信息，这也是一种风格。而新的译文则注重总体风格的翻译。

对比之后，读者普遍觉得英文（原文）显得直白，不如译文(中文)典雅，读者的感受恐怕首先与中、英文风格不同有关，中文译文实则是对原文理解之后的再创造，而不是简单的“对等”翻译。其新译不是逐字对译（word for word），用“浮世”来译“in this world”不仅显得简练、大气、形象，音韵也好，其意境也显得深邃并扩大了读者想象的空间。浮世指人间，人世。旧时认为人世间是浮沉聚散不定的，故有“浮生若梦”之说。这样译也体现了我国译界老翻译家们提倡的要发挥译文（这里指中文）优势的论点。

总觉得这首诗的汉译有仿古风的风格，这跟滴水不漏地译好每个字的译风大相径庭。可见，译诗只在每个单字、单词或每行语句上下功夫是不够的。必须着眼于一首诗的全局意境和风格的再创造。

我们若把“Even if from another world, still love you till the end of time”译为“就算来自不同世界，依旧爱你到时间的尽头”，似乎与原文很“等值”，但远不如译成“就算来自不同世界，依旧爱你到地老天荒”更受读者欢迎。

关于文学翻译，我国历来有“神似”“形似”统一、“形神兼备”的提法——简单明了地概括了我国诗歌翻译的理论与实践。

【注释】

（1）英译白居易《赋得古原草送别》、辛弃疾《采桑子》、陈子昂《登幽州台歌》、吴绛雪《春》、唐寅《我爱秋香》（藏头诗）均见朱曼华《中国历代诗词英译集锦》。

（2）英译李煜《相见欢》见朱曼华《李煜诗词英译全集》。

Translator's Postscript

In August 2008, the editorial department of *Chinese Translators Journal* once gave me an opportunity to attend the 18th International Federation of Translators. Since then, I have further strengthened my sense of mission to let Chinese culture go global to influence human future, and started to translate Chinese poetry into English systematically. The Commercial Press International Co., Ltd. has published *Chinese Famous Poetry Translated by Manfield Zhu, Complete Collection of Li Yu's Poetry*, and Blossom Press of China International Publishing Group published *Zhao Puchu's Anthology of the Tea Culture translated by Manfield Zhu*. These translation works were republished after the first edition , and one of them for the third time, all of which are welcome by readers both at home and abroad.

Translating poetry is always a bittersweet and a regrettable thing for me. Sometimes even the translation draft was revised more than once, I was still not satisfied with myself. When the version was just published, I might be happy for a little while, but a few years later there would be even more dissatisfactory points and even I'd like to retranslate it. This kind of really a secret pain would make my mind restless, almost all my life. Of course, there were few times when translation was smooth, I wouldn't like to change a word again.

During 10 years, three of my translation works heve been published. I am very grateful to the Commercial International Co., Ltd. and Blossom Press of China International Publishing Group for making my long-cherished wish come true. If no authoritative presses gave me an opportunity to translate and introduce traditional Chinese culture to the wider world, I would make no full use of my English as a specialty.

I know I am quite ambitious but I am weak, still I will not give up my original intention. I hope I can work hard to overcome my clumsiness and continue to work hard to improve myself in translating quality.

Now I would like to take this opportunity to show readers some poems translated into English. I really want to hear different voices. No one is perfect, no gold is perfect, a translator is limited of capability. No translator should be too confident of his own works. I hope I will have enough courage to bring with my translation works to go over the high wall of the academy to face the world poetic pals.

In this paper, a few self-translated poems are quoted:

A Farewell Poem to the Old Meadow
Bai Juyi (772 ~ 846)
离离原上草，一岁一枯荣。
野火烧不尽，春风吹又生。
远芳侵古道，晴翠接荒城。
又送王孙去，萋萋满别情。

Grass is spreading over the meadow,
Life or death will yearly come, yearly go.
The bale-fire can burn away the green,
Spring breeze will help it survive again.
The sweet green afar intrudes the old way,
The waste town meets it on a sunny day.
Seeing off my bosom friend again,
Still I feel strongly reluctant in pain.

The rhyming scheme between Chinese and English is different, but there are still some analogies. In general, the rhyming scheme of English poetry is similar to Chinese if there are four or more adjacent lines to form a poem. That is, (1) the first and second lines rhyme, the third and fourth lines rhyme (AABB), (2) the second and fourth lines rhyme (the first and third lines do not have to rhyme, which is similar to a Chinese saying—an ancient-style Chinese poetry— “whether line 1,3 and 5 rhyme or not rhyme is both okay, but line 2,4 and 6 should rhyme one another” (ABCB), (3) the first line and third lines rhyme, the second and fourth lines rhyme (ABAB), (4) line 1 and line 4 rhyme; line 2 and line 3 rhyme (ABBA).

Poet Bai Juyi used "AABB" -rhyming scheme in his *A Farewell Poem to the Old Meadow*. Bai Juyi's *Long Poem on Eternal Grief* in Chinese rhyme is also in "AABB" rhyming scheme. The steps, iambus and rhyme of the English translation generally conform to the standards of English poetry. I try to avoid consonant ending words as the final rhyme, in order to have better sound. The final two lines of *A Farewell Poem to the Old Meadow* in English translation are "again" and "pain", respectively. They are easy to read and sounds good.

Please read aloud the following two lines to end Poet Bai Juyi's above poem:

Seeing off my bosom friend again,
Still I feel strongly reluctant in pain.

The translation of *A Farewell Poem to the Old Meadow* was selected in "51 test. net"(无忧考网), and posted in the column — "home · English translation qualification examination · navigation · preparation for examination" (09-24-2008).

According to the structure, Chinese vowels can be divided into single vowel, double vowel and nasal vowel — there are 39 finals in Mandarin speech. Chinese complex vowels consist of the vowel head, the vowel body, and the vowel tail. Only one Chinese nasal-vowel followed by consonant n or ng. But English has more words with this kind of consonant letters. This feature of Chinese phonetic rhyme enlarges the choice for translators to deal with the translation of Chinese poetry into English. Because much more English words are ended up with consonant letters that far exceed their vowels (a, e, i, o, u). For this reason, it is easier for translators to find the appropriate rhyme words according to the words contained in the translation.

In the Tang dynasty, Bai Juyi wrote a poem, *Long Poem on Eternal Grief*. Almost all of the original texts were rhymed by two adjacent lines — AABB or ABBA, and occasionally

ABAB or ABCB. Therefore, the translator can strive to be similar with the final rhyme of original text, which can narrow the metrical differences between the two languages. *Long Poem on Eternal Grief* has a total of 120 lines. Here only a few lines of English translation are selected for reference to friends who are interested in English translation.

Long Poem on Eternal Grief
Bai Juyi (772~846)
天生丽质难自弃，一朝选在君王侧。
回眸一笑百媚生，六宫粉黛无颜色。

Rhyming scheme [AABB]
Her natural beauty could hardly keep her inside,
Once she was selected to the lust monarch's side.
Glancing back with a smile of 100-times charming,
She let six-palace imperial beauties no good-looking.

云鬓花颜金步摇，芙蓉帐暖度春宵。
春宵苦短日高起，从此君王不早朝。

Rhyming scheme [AABB]
Her phoenix coronet with a hairpin Gold Pendant,
She spent spring night to shelter in warm lotus tent.
Spring night was too short to stop daybreak,
The Emperor could not go for timely work.

揽衣推枕起徘徊，珠箔银屏迤逦开。
云鬓半偏新睡觉，花冠不整下堂来。

Rhyming scheme [ABAB]
Getting up to put on her gown to push pillow aside,
She rolled up to have bead-curtain screen open.
Just awoken, her temples hairs inclined to one side,
She left from her bedroom with her coronet bun.

How to realize the beauty of intonation? Different translators have different ideas. If it is possible to make the final rhyme of the English translation contain English words equivalent to the pronunciation of Chinese antecedent complex vowels— (ai, ao, ei, ou) , then, the rhyming sounds pleasant. In some English words, it is not difficult for the translator to seek for the so-called Chinese antecedent complex vowels, such as the following words— fly, die, why, cow, law, way, stay, go, low and so on.

Joyful Reunion
Li Yu (937~ 978)
无言独上西楼，月如钩，
寂寞梧桐深院锁清秋。
剪不断，理还乱，是离愁。
别是一番滋味在心头。

Upstairs, voicelessly I'd like to go,
The moon is like a bow,
The deep courtyard can hold,
Lonely parasol tree to lock autumn cold.
It is impossible to cut off my sorrow,
I comb it up but fail,
No way to cancel my parting sorrow,
In my heart it's a tasteful farewell.

Picking Mulberry

Xin Qiji (1140~1207)

少年不识愁滋味，爱上层楼。
爱上层楼，为赋新词强说愁。
而今识尽愁滋味，欲说还休。
欲说还休，却道天凉好个秋。

As a young fellow,
I did not know the taste of sorrow,
I'd like to go,
To the high watchtower from the low.
I'd like to go,
To the high watchtower from the low,
I was on purpose to say "sorrow",
For writing a new poem.
Now I know how about the sorrow,
But I don't want to say what I know.
Now I know how about the sorrow,
But I don't want to say what I know,
I just talk something about the autumn cold.

The final rhyme can only be chosen according to the situation and the possibility provided by the original text. However, the translator can consciously seek for much more ideal sound and rhyme by adjusting word order, changing synonyms, and making full use of English morphological way.

Xin Qiji's *Picking Mulberry* in English was welcome by the graduate students studying the comparative literature at Communication University of China. In some primary schools,

English teachers also read it aloud to pupils in English class.

It is really worth mentioning that the translated poems can be served for teaching or enjoying.

After editing and publishing the few of my translated works, I experienced the ups and downs of the translation. I did not dare to say which translation was the best, but I could not forget the poems that were most thoughtful and familiar to the readers. I feel it's difficult to find an appropriate, proper translation for Li Qingzhao's *Sounds Go Glow,* and difficult to translate it quite well just once. Ten years later, I feel something unsatisfactory when I read the version translated ten years ago. As time goes on, I must generate some new ideas, not only because I have made progress in English, but also because of the better understanding of the original text, for instance, at the very beginning, I think the word "late" used to describe the time was right, but after reading an authoritative commentator Yu Pingbo's "early morning or dawn", I want to change my original version.

One of poetess Li Qingzhao's famous Song-poems with 14 overlapping words such as "寻寻觅觅" attracted scholars for thousands of years. In modern times, people have been more and more interested in discussing how to translate this kind of folded words. Some emphasize the "transliteration", while others advocate imitating the rhyme pattern of English initial rhyme. In this paper, the author does not want to be satisfied with the translation of "by means of duplication". Because Chinese translators often unconsciously ignore that it is not English's strong point to use the overlapping words as frequently as Chinese. The Chinese people tend to think in Chinese thinking way instead of English native speaker's thinking way. However, English native speakers or readers do not like that. They are familiar with "long long ago" "very very good", but not used in Chinglish way— "good good study" "day day up", which just let them laugh off. Perhaps, no one would like to translate "days and nights" into "day day night night"; no one would capsize a boat in such a small river. As a Chinese translator, he must enhance his English sense instead of Chinese to take careful consideration of English grammatical structure.

Now let me show readers a flexible way to translate such an overlapping word structure as follows:

寻寻觅觅，冷冷清清，凄凄惨惨戚戚。

I am to seek, seek and look for what I think,
I feel cold, lonely, so sad and so tragic,
To be sorrowful, unhappy and lovesick.

In general, the subject of authentic English is not omitted, except in imperative or spoken language or in a specific context. When translating an English sentence, or a poetic line, it is often necessary to add its logical subject.

In a word, if the translator's English sense is not enough to give you the courage, do not use the overlapping way reluctantly.

Native speakers prefer to use English alliterative fashion instead. For instance, "You drink, you drive, and you die", a series of words (verbs, nouns, adjectives, etc.) that begin with the three consonants "d" and end with the vowel sound.

The literati also had a good feeling for the rhetoric of rhyming— two or more alliterative words in a string that sounded catchy and sweet.

We should try this alliterative fashion instead. "lovely posture and light manner", for example, can be used to translate Du Mu's "娉娉袅袅" in his 7-character metrical poem *the Farewell*:

娉娉袅袅十三余，豆蔻梢头二月初。
春风十里扬州路，卷上珠帘总不如。

She is 13 years old in lovely posture and light manner,
She looks like February young cardamom top flower.
Spring breeze blows 10-Li Yangzhou's street maiden,

No one could match her beauty within pearl curtain.

In the course of cultural exchange between Chinese and western poetry, it is necessary for a translator to master all kinds of poetry, including some special one, such as palindromic and acrostic poems and so on, which will attract more and more poetic fans to appreciate different poetic styles. How to translate the Chinese palindromic poetry is worth to have a try.

Since the Song dynasty, the palindromic poetry has been like a strange army alone standing up to march on. Such a peculiar verse in higher level could reflect the superiority of the Chinese language. There have long been misconceptions about palindromes. Some thought that they were the product of the idle classes or the scholar-officials. Their value were often artificially devalued and rarely translated. At present, with China's national strength rising, westerners have begun to take the initiative to learn Chinese. Learning some palindromic poems would play a stimulant role to students, at this time, they will be more aware of the concept of teaching through entertainment.

The appearance of palindromic poetry is closely related to the flexible sequence and the flexible character of Chinese language. Also, because Chinese is a non-morphological language, there is no complicated change of suffix, verb form, gender, and so on. Therefore, it is easy to create the flexible word order, which can help write more palindromic poems. The scientific and flexible Chinese word order is the natural hotbed for developing palindromic poems.

Here are two palindromic poems translated from Chinese into English in palindromic way, the poem can be read either in backward way or in forward way.

The given 10 Chinese characters could create a 4-line with 28 characters:

Spring
Wu Jiangxue（1650~1674）
(Palindromic Poem)

莺啼岸柳弄春晴，
柳弄春晴晓月明。
明月晓晴春弄柳，
晴春弄柳岸啼莺。

Crowing warblers in willow, help spring glow,
To help spring glow, at dawn, the moon bright.
Bright moon at dawn, glow spring helps willow,
Glow spring helps the willow warbler crow.

The ten words of the poem “warbler-crow- willow - help - spring - glow - dawn - moon - bright” can be read according to a structure formula of the palindromic way, that is, a given word order like this:

1 2 3 4 5 6 7~
4 5 6 7 8 9 10~
10 9 8 7 6 5 4~
7 6 5 4 3 2 1>

Colored Autumn
Tang Yin (1470~1523)
(Palindromic Poem)
悠云白雁过南楼，
雁过南楼半色秋。
秋色半楼南过雁，
楼南过雁白云悠。

Leisurely clouds, white geese fly south pavilion,
White geese fly south pavilion in half autumn.
Autumn half in pavilion south, fly white geese,

Pavilion south fly geese in white leisurely clouds.

Tang Yin is not only a writer of the palindrome, but also a good writer of acrostic poems. As a literary talent, once he wrote an acrostic poem to a girl named 秋香 (Autumn Fragrant), so the title of his acrostic poem was *I love Autumn Fragrant*. His writings were full of extraordinary literary skills, very natural and fluent without any trace of being too delicate and contrived.

I Love Autumn Fragrant

Tang Yin（1470~1523）

(Acrostic Poem)

我画蓝江水悠悠，
爱晚亭上枫叶愁。
秋月溶溶照佛寺，
香烟袅袅绕经楼。

I painted the blue river slowly and slowly to flow,
Love-Evening-Kiosk is to hold maples' sorrow.
Autumn moonlight is hovering Buddha temple,
Fragrant incense-smoke's curling up Sutra Hall.

The translation of this poem was approved by translator Mr. Jiang Feng. His translation theory is the "combination of form and content".

In the Tang Dynasty, Chen Zi'ang (661~702) wrote a poem *Stepping upon Youzhou-Watchtower*.

Poet Chen's poem consists of two lines of five words (words here used to refer Chinese characters) and two lines of six words, no matter what kind of poetry they were like, they were not restrained by the pattern of poetry, and they were not coincident with any kind of the rhyming style. For thousands of years, all the people are proud of it.

It can be seen that no matter writing or translating poems, the content and the form of expression should have no essence to be lost. The above-mentioned poem may not be in line with the standard of poems, but it is popular and unwearied.

Stepping upon Youzhou-Watchtower
Chen Zi'ang (661~702)
前不见古人，
后不见来者。
念天地之悠悠，
独怆然而涕下！

Looking ahead, I could find no ancient man,
Glancing back, no one coming forth was seen.
I pondered my motherland so wide, so open,
My tears burst out as I watched the heaven.

All of the above mentioned English translations are of classical poetry, mainly focused on the so-called sound beauty and form beauty. In my opinion, how to achieve the translation of meaning beauty has fewer theoretic arguments and more consensuses.

But how to embody this "faithful to original text" or "loyalty" still need to do more practice in detailed discussion, and that's also not so easy. Almost all the translation works can tell readers the translator's translation skills to deal with the so-called meaning or sense beauty or what the translator has done around the idea of beauty or likeness.

Great writer Lu Xun's *From the Writing to the Article* has a paragraph on Three Beauties' conclusion: the so-called "meaning beauty", which refers to the heartfelt sense with feeling as the first point; the "sound beauty" means to beautify the ears as the second point; the "form beauty" means to beautify the eyes as the third point. Lu Xun's assertion of "three beauties" may have a certain foresight to the construction of literary translation theory in the translation circle.

Recently a short lyric poem is quite popular and favorable, which is a dialogue in American female writer Stephanie Meyer's novel entitled *The Twilight Saga*. At the age of 27 (in 1999), she started writing the novel series of *The Twilight Saga* and her novel was adapted into a movie in 2008,from which some brilliant quotes or dialogues spread over the world. One of them is like this:

I love three things in this world,
The sun, the moon and you.
The sun for the day,
The moon for the night,
And you forever.

A new translation of this poem is as follows:
浮世三千，吾爱有三，
日，月与卿；
日为朝，月为暮，
卿为朝朝暮暮。
（网上的一种新译文，译者不详）

The very short lyric poem might be quoted from William Michael Rossetti (1829~1919) who wrote "Life of John Keats" in 1887 as follows:

For the world you may just be somebody,
But for somebody you maybe the world.
I love three things, the sun the moon and you.
The sun for the day,

The moon for the night,

And you forever.

Here is the old chinese translation to “Life of John Keats”:

对于世界而言，你也许只是某个人，

但对某个人而言，你或许就是整个世界。

我热爱三个事物，太阳，月亮和你。

太阳给我白昼，月亮给我夜晚，

而你，给我永远。（佚名译）

By contrast, the old Chinese translation seemed to be a literal translation, plain, natural like a flying cloud or running water without deliberately exaggerating or shortening the information, which is also a good style, and the new translation is simulated in a classic poetic style.

After comparison, readers generally think that English (original) is more straightforward and less elegant than the translated version (Chinese), and readers' feelings may first be related to the differences in Chinese and English styles — the Chinese translation is based on actually a re-creation theory after understanding the original text, rather than the simple “equivalence” translation.

Its new translation is not in word-for-word way, and the phrase “in this world” translated into “floating world” is not only concise, open-minded, vivid and rigorous, but also profound to enlarge the space of readers' imagination. Floating World (world of mortals) means the human world. In the old days, people thought that the world was floating and unsteady. Such translation also reflects the arguments that the Chinese aged translators advocated to play Chinese advantages in an important role of translation.

I always think such a Chinese translation of this poem is of an archaistic style, it is different from the style of translating in word-for-word way. Therefore, it is not enough to translate a poem only by careful consideration of each word, or each line. The translator must focus on the overall artistic conception and the re-creation of the style.

Another example for understanding the style of the translated poem:

"Even if from another world, still love you till the end of time."

（A）"就算来自不同世界，依旧爱你到时间的尽头。"

（B）"就算来自不同世界，依旧爱你到天荒地老。"

"Even if you come from different world, still love you till the Heaven will turn barren and the earth will grow old."

It is clear that "love you till the end of time" is concise but "love you till the Heaven will turn barren and the earth will grow old" is full of imagination. Maybe the Chinese young guys are a little bit interested in this version (B) that is like a vivid picture to leave a rather deep impression of love.